PUB W

IN SOM

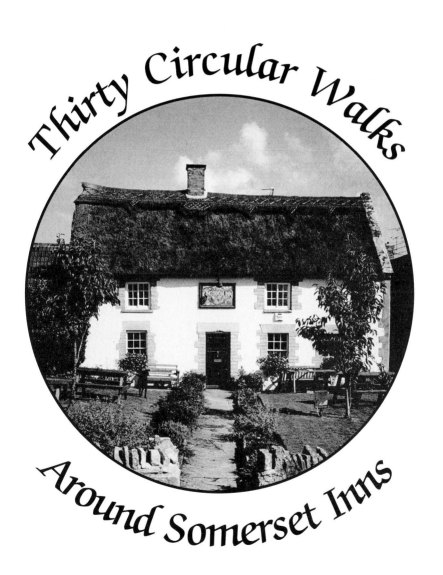

Thirty Circular Walks
Around Somerset Inns

Mike Power

Other publications in the series

"Pub Walks in Dorset"
"Forty More Pub Walks in Dorset"
"Pub Walks in Hampshire & I.O.W."
"Pub Walks in West Sussex"
"Pub Walks in East Sussex"
"Pub Walks in Devon"
"Pub Walks in Cornwall"
"Pub Walks in the New Forest"
"Pub Walks in Hardy's Wessex"
"Pub Walks in Kent"

Ist edition published Nov 1998

ACKNOWLEDGEMENTS
In writing this book I am indebted to Gill Coombes who accompanied me on several occasions, to David Hancock who recommended some good pubs, and to the many licensees for their assistance.

1 Clayford Ave
Ferndown
Dorset. BH22 9PQ

ISBN 1 898073155

Publishers note
Whilst every care has been taken to ensure that all the information contained in this book is correct neither the authors or publishers can accept any responsibility for any inaccuracies that occur

Printed by: Pardy & Son (Printers) Ltd., Ringwood, Hampshire
Photographs: Mike Power
Front cover: Kingsdon Inn, Kingsdon
Back cover: The Rock Inn, Waterrow

INTRODUCTION

Somerset has long been one of my favourite counties so writing this book has not only been a great pleasure but confirmed fully my love of the area. It is a County of great contrasts ranging from bleak moorland and beautiful bluebell forests to rugged coastlines and peaceful holiday beaches. Vast areas of wet lowland are in stark contrast to the rolling hills of Quantock, Mendip, Brendon and Blackdown whilst between the large towns are some of the smallest and most beautiful villages to found anywhere in England. It is in these areas that we have concentrated the majority of our walks. All the inns have been chosen for their charm or accessibility to a good walk no charge is made for inclusion in this book.

The walks are all circular, vary in length from 2 miles to $7\frac{1}{2}$ and are explained in detail with an accompanying sketch map. They should appeal not only to people perhaps walking for the first time but to the more experienced rambler. They are designed to start and finish at the pub with the incentive of lunch or a drink at the end but there is nothing to stop you starting anywhere along the route. It is assumed that you will want to visit the pub but on the rare occasion you do not I would respectfully ask you not to use their car park. Where possible I have listed suitable alternatives.

The Countryside Commission set a target to have all the 130,000 miles of 'rights of way' in England and Wales in good order by the millennium. Whilst I found certain areas in the County very well sign-posted and all paths clearly marked in other instances it was impossible to even find the path. All problems have been reported in the hope that by the time of publication all the paths will be accessible and clearly marked.

The new 'Rights of Way Act', which came in to force on August 13th 1990, has much improved the rights of ramblers; it was a massive step forward in path protection. The Act requires occupiers who disturb the land to make good the surface within 24 hours of the disturbance or 2 weeks if the disturbance is the first one for a particular crop. Where no width is recorded the minimum for a path must be 1 metre and 2 metres for a bridleway and the exact line of the path must be apparent on the ground. Furthermore the occupier must prevent crops growing on, or encroaching onto the path.

Any person using a public footpath has the right to remove as much of the obstruction as necessary to allow him or her to pass, but not to cause wilful damage to property. If the obstruction cannot be removed the walker is entitled to leave the path and walk round it, causing no more damage than is necessary. If the path has been sown with crops you are entitled to follow the route even if it means treading on the crop. You should report any problems you find to the relevant rights of way department.

It is always advisable to carry an Ordnance Survey map with you. The Landranger series has a scale of 1:50 000, $1\frac{1}{4}$ inch to the mile. The five you will require covering this book are Nos. 172, 181, 182, 183 and 193.

It has now been proved that walking is extremely good for you, it can also be safe providing a few simple rules are observed. Wear suitable clothing, lightweight quick drying or waterproof trousers are advisable, as many paths become overgrown in summer. A waterproof jacket or cagoule is an essential item so too are strong waterproof well-treaded boots. Where safe to do so keep to the right-hand side of the road in the absence of pavements. A compass can be useful also a torch, a whistle, fresh water and a mobile phone if you have one. I always carry a stick it is ideal for clearing brambles, testing the stability of the ground ahead and can be waived in the air to deter animals.

Wherever you go in the countryside, always follow the code. Do not light fires, fasten all gates, keep dogs under control and always on a lead where livestock are present. Take your litter home, do not pick wild flowers or dig up plants.

I very much enjoyed all these walks I hope you will too.

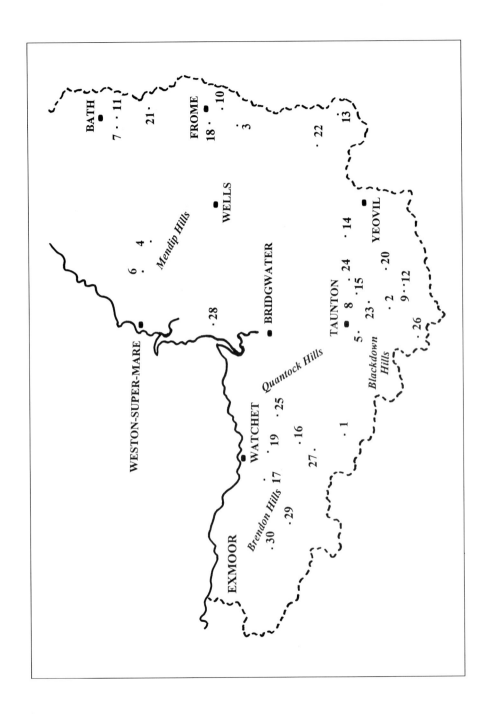

BATH

7 ·· 11

21·

FROME

18 · ● · 10

· 3

· 22

13

WELLS

Mendip Hills

· 4

6 ·

YEOVIL

· 14

BRIDGWATER

· 24

· 20

TAUNTON

· 15

9·· 12

· 28

· 8

· 2

23·

· 26

5·

Blackdown Hills

WESTON-SUPER-MARE

Quantock Hills

·25

· 1

WATCHET

· 19

·16

27·

Brendon Hills 17

· 29

EXMOOR

· 30

The Globe Inn, Appley

Overlooking open fields within a web of narrow country lanes, this five hundred year old welcoming inn remains unspoilt and totally in keeping with its very rural surroundings. Three comfortable rustically furnished rooms radiate off the narrow stone-flagged entrance passage that leads to the small serving hatch. The 'Front Room' has a small servery in one wall whilst the aptly named 'Top Room' has various prints of liners and a collection of models displayed in a large case on the wall. Families are welcome in the 'Man's Kitchen', which has a low bowed ceiling, part wood panelled walls, assorted memorabilia and polished brass. All three rooms have open fires There is also has a good skittle alley and large rear beer garden with a small children's play area.

The inn is a freehouse very well run by the owners. Real ales presently include the Cotleigh Tawny plus a changing guest ale.

Excellent food can be had all week 12–2 and 7–10 (Sunday 9.30). Heading the list are starters such as home-made fish soup, chef's chicken liver pate – made with cream and cognac and prawn othello – a light cold egg pancake filled with prawns, celery and pineapple. An interesting choice of main meals include half a crispy coated duckling served with a sweet chilli, plum and spring onion sauce and breast of local chicken stuffed with pine nuts, bacon, raisins and apricots, oven roasted and served with a Madeira sauce. There are fish dishes, a Sunday roast, meals for children and a vegetarian selection; one dish being spinach and pasta cooked with sweet corn, mushrooms and cream topped with melted Stilton. Supplementing the menu are daily specials which on my last visit included cream of fennel and potato soup, fresh whole lemon sole, Hungarian pork – cubes of pork cooked with onions, peppers, mushrooms, red wine, paprika and sour cream and beef bolognaise served on a bed of tagliatelle with Parmesan cheese

Weekday opening times 11–2.30 & 6.30–11. Sunday 12–3 & 7–10.30. Closed Monday lunch times except bank holidays

Families welcome but no dogs.

Telephone: (01823) 672327.

Remotely situated Appley lies 4 miles west of Wellington best reached from the A38 at Sand Pit. From the motorway leave at junction 27.

Approximate distance: 4¾ miles. OS Map 181 ST 072/215.

Good car park at the rear also limited parking in lane outside.

A very enjoyable walk mostly on field paths and peaceful country lanes exploring the area west of Appley and twice crosses the River Tone. The walk is scenic, not over demanding and apart from the areas around the farms generally good underfoot.

Turn left from the inn and almost immediately cross the stile into the field on the right. Keeping close to the hedge walk down to the bottom, over the stile beside the gate and carry on down to the next stile signposted River. Maintain direction down to the gate then bear right across to the stile and straight ahead to the stile beside the gate. Turn right crossing the attractive stone bridge over the River Tone an area abundant with wild flowers. Cross one more stile then turn right into the lane.

Walk round past the entrance to Cothay Manor and join the signed footpath on the left just prior to the bend. Keep straight ahead beside the gully on the left walk to the far side and pick up the farm entance into the lane and straight ahead bearing left up the bank to the stile. (footpath signposted) Keep straight ahead along the wide

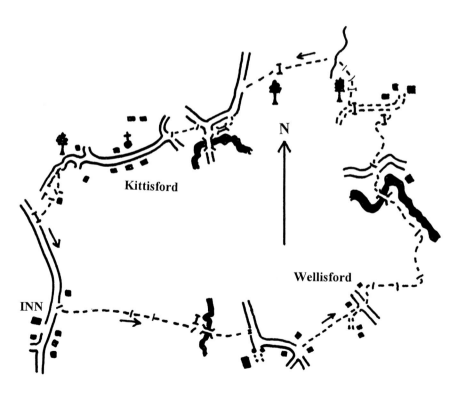

River Tone

sunken track, cross the stile ahead and follow the fence (ignoring the stile on the right) round to meet the stile on the left. Cross into the field and bearing left follow the field boundary down to the stile at the bottom, climb into the field on the left and keep to the riverside path (good place to see snowdrops) up to the bridge and along the path to the lane.

Walk straight across and over the stile into the field opposite. Keeping close to the hedge walk all the way round, up to the farm gate, through onto the farm road and turn left. After passing through the gate turn immediately right and follow the hedge line up to the gate in the far corner and straight ahead to the crossing point in the corner. Go over into the field, across the stream and round the field following the hedge towards the wood. Pass through the gate into the adjoing field and make your way left to pick up the track leading to the farm. Pass to the left, go out into the lane and turn left.

At the end of the lane join the raised path on the left, cross the small bridge, turn right into the lane and almost immediately climb the stile into the field on the left. Bearing right cross to the stile in the far hedge, go over into the lane and keep straight ahead to the village of Kittisford. Follow the lane out of the village, down then up the hill walking as far as the stile on the left. Bearing right go up to the stile in the wire fence, cross the track, over the stile opposite then bear right making for the farm gate, through into the lane and turn left back along this attractive lane to the pub.

Square & Compass, Ashill

There are views of the Blackdown Hills from the front of this two-storey roadside inn attractively draped with creepers in summer. The bar, heated by an open log fire in an attractive brick fireplace, has a beamed ceiling, carpeted floor and assorted furniture, which includes a large wooden settle. There is a separate dining room, seating at the front and more in the garden.

The pub is a freehouse recently taken over and personally run by the new owners Chris and Janet Slow. Real ales presently available on hand pump include Exmoor Ale, Wadworth 6X and Flowers plus beers from Branscombe and the local Moor Beer Company.

Food is available 12 noon onwards and from 7 till late. Apart from specials such as celery and Stilton soup, cauliflower cheese topped with either mushrooms or bacon, a mild lamb curry and Mediterranean pork braised with red wine, sundried tomatoes and herbs, the set menu lists deep fried mushrooms and crudite also king prawns in hot garlic butter and deep fried brie. The choice of main dishes is good ranging from a farmhouse grill and breaded cod to a large omelette and vegetarian mushroom stroganoff. There is a good range of pasta dishes, steaks and fish options like seafood crepes consisting of scallops, mussels, prawns and calamari. Old favourites such as locally made sausage, egg and chips and ham, egg and chips are printed alongside Thai chicken curry and prawn and halloumi cheese stir-fry. Sandwiches, ploughman's and jacket potatoes are available for those just wanting a snack. Separate children's menu, Sunday roast plus various sweets and coffee.

Children in family room, no objection to dogs.

Self-catering holiday accommodation sleeps up to 6.

Weekday opening times 12–3 & 6.30–11, Sunday 12–3 & 7–10.30

Telephone: (01823) 480487.

Walk No. 2

Take the turning for Windmill Hill signed by Stewley Cross garage off the A358. north from its junction with the A303.

Approximate distance: $7\frac{1}{2}$ miles. OS Map 193 ST 310/167.

Park at the pub or in the road at the front.

A long challenging, strenuous but enjoyable walk on field and woodland paths, country lanes and grass and gravel bridleways. One of the best features is the woodland path from Curland Common, which takes you high up to Castle Neroche, an early settlement. As it can be extremely wet and muddy in the winter try and walk from May onwards especially when the bluebells should be at their best.

Turn right from the pub, and after passing a pair of cottages take the footpath on the left sign-posted, Barrington Hill 1. Walk down to the gate, cross the river and go up the field to the stile in the top corner. Continue ahead until you reach the stile and plank bridge on the right then walk up the field beside the hedge to the stile at the top

maintaining direction across two more fields finally over the stile into the lane.

Turn right, round the bend and at the next bend take the track on the left. Just before reaching the dwelling go through the little gate on the right, across to a similar one then follow the path to the right which winds its way through this lovely wild flower

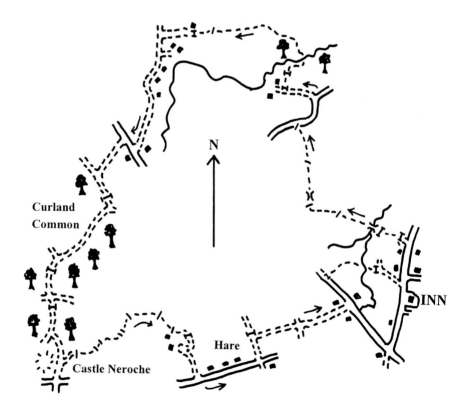

filled copse down to the stream. Carefully cross and climb the bank, enter the field and bear left up beside the boundary making for the gap in the corner. Keep straight ahead to the stile, through the orchard and out through the gate onto the track. Keep straight ahead until you reach the wide grass bridleway on the left, which will eventually bring you out into the road by Newtown Farm.

Turn right and further on take the signed bridleway track on the left. Turn left at the cross track, pass round the gate and join the trail on the right. This often muddy but very attractive track, home to numerous wild flowers rises steadily, crosses a ditch, narrows then widens. Ignore the track on the right but continue climbing, through the gate into the bluebell wood. Cross the farm track, enter the bluebell wood opposite and part way up fork left. The path climbs very steeply from this point through a gully eventually reaching the viewpoint at Castle Neroche. Welcome seating is provided together with a notice board giving the history of the area. It is believed to have been a small defended settlement some 2600 years ago. Covering 72 hectares the woods surrounding the hill form part of the main forest within the Blackdown Hill area.

Retrace your steps following the red ringed posts only as far as the gully then keep to the rim on the right, go up onto the top of the hill and round to the stile on the right. Walk beside the hedge, cross a pair of stiles on the left and follow the boundary round to a similar pair on the left. Go down the field to the stile in the fence then bear right, down and across the hillside making for the distant stile in the corner. Cross the field bearing right, through the gateway and down to the stile beside the hay barn then bear left down the field. Just past the pond go through the gate on the right, up through the farmyard and along the track, out into the lane and turn left.

Many wild flowers have established themselves along this very peaceful lane which passes through Hare. Keep walking until you reach the track on the left leading to Swaddles Green Farm. When you reach the gate turn right. Ownership of this wide drove track, known locally as 'Long Drove' is uncertain and although not shown to be an official right of way is regularly used by both riders and walkers alike. After passing the farm you can either turn right then next left back to the pub or to avoid this often busy and fast road turn left and join a footpath on the right, un-signed when I was last here but hopefully is now. Walk for a while and upon reaching a gate on the right (opposite a large oak) pass through into the field. Keeping close to the hedge on the right, walk to the end, cross the stream into the field opposite, head up to the gate and join the grass track beyond leading directly to the pub.

The Three Horseshoes Inn, Batcombe

Formally known as the Batcombe Inn and now under new ownership this out of the way pub, located in a narrow lane beside the village church is a little gem. The rear entrance is through a pretty honeysuckle covered arch and across a tub filled patio. The one very attractive beamed bar is heated by warm log fires one of which is set in a large inglenook fireplace. The carpeted green floor perfectly compliments the terracotta rag washed and stencilled walls. Furnishings consist of farmhouse tables, tub chairs and padded window seats. There is a separate stone walled dining room, a large beer garden and children's play area.

This extremely well run inn is a freehouse owned by West Country Village Inns Ltd. Real ales listed are Wadworth 6X, Butcombe Bitter and Batemans XB.

Available everyday 12–2 and 7–9 (9.30 Saturday), the excellent food is well above average and nicely presented. The lunchtime menu lists savoury stuffed mushrooms and double baked cheese souffle served with a basil sauce together with more substantial dishes like local herby pork sausages, pan fired salmon served on a bed of leeks and tomato stuffed with wild rice, aubergine and herbs topped with welsh rarebit. There are five starters on the supper menu including crab ravioli in a ginger scented chicken broth, followed by crispy belly pork cooked in white wine on a bed of tomatoes and onions with flageolet beans, roast rack of lamb with a pepper crust served with its juices on minted mash and monkfish roulade stuffed with a duxelle of mushrooms and served with a rocket sauce. The specials board, changed daily, recently listed avocado salad with spicy crab mayonnaise, confit of duck with onion gravy and stir fried chicken with egg noodles, shredded vegetables, and black bean sauce. Sweets range from orange burnt cream and individual sticky toffee pudding with clotted cream to strawberry pavlova and gooseberry and elderflower fool served with an almond tuille.

Weekday opening times, 11.30–3 & 6–11. Sunday 12–3 & 7–10.30.

Children and dogs equally welcome.

Telephone: (01373) 820696.

Village signed north of Bruton from the A359.

Approximate distance: $4\frac{1}{4}$ miles. OS Map 183 ST 690/391.

Park behind the pub, in the lane or the small lay-by opposite the church.

An enjoyable, slightly challenging scenic walk through Batcombe Vale on peaceful lanes and field paths at one point passing close to the River Altham. Although generally good underfoot the going can be a bit strenuous especially in summer when some paths can become very overgrown.

Leave the pub and walk back down the lane, turn right and after a few steps enter the field on the left sign-posted, to Portway Hill. Make your way straight ahead to the crossing point and bear left down the steep field path to the crossing point, go out into the lane and turn right. Walk up the hill and turn left into Moor Lane. This peaceful roadway rises steadily before veering to the right at which point turn left up the short track and immediately join the path on the right (can be overgrown). Walk up to the crossing point, bear right across to the stile and climb the field bearing right up to the gate. Go straight across, through the gap in the hedge opposite maintaining direction to the gate then turn right into the lane.

Walk for about a quarter of a mile along this attractive lane, its hedgerows crammed in spring with many wild flowers including

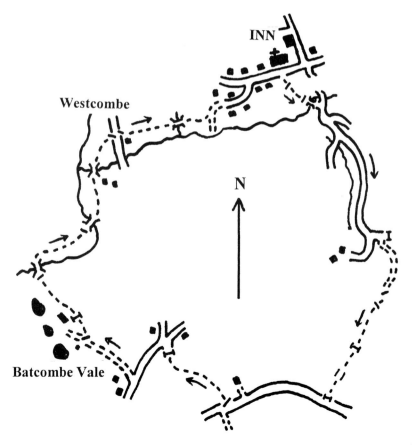

swathes of blue meadow crane's-bill. After passing the dwelling on the right cross the stile into the field on the right and, keeping close to the hedge walk round to the gate on the far side, go out into the lane and turn left.

Keep to the highway as far as the farm buildings then turn right into the drive and go down towards the caravan site. Many wild flowers have colonised this track. I noticed horseradish, geraniums and wild monkshood to name but a few. At the bottom climb the stile into the field on the right and bear left across to the gate. Continue ahead up the rise and down to the stile in the bottom corner, cross the bridge and turn right into the field.

Keep straight ahead, the river away on your right and walk round to the bridge in the small wood. It is an attractive spot with two small waterfalls and filled with garlic smelling ransoms. Cross into the field and keep straight ahead bearing left opposite the buildings. Join the grass track, which passes in front of the cattle shed leading to a concrete bridge, go over into the field and make your way to the stile on the right.

Cross the lane to the stile opposite and follow the path ahead close to the river. After crossing a bridge the path passes through an attractive wood with yet more garlic ransoms. Bear left up the track then go right, past the dwellings, out into the lane turning right back past the church to the pub.

Blagdon Lake

The New Inn, Blagdon

Set in the heart of the Mendips with spectacular views of Blagdon Lake this very atmospheric and comfortably furnished inn has a carpeted and low beamed main bar on two levels dominated by a massive inglenook fireplace. A large curved wooden settle is ideally placed for cosy winter evenings where one can warm oneself by open log fires throughout the winter. A large collection of horse brasses are displayed over the fireplace and hanging from the beams together with other metallic paraphernalia. A second smaller, carpeted bar has a large stone fireplace and open grate. There is a piano in one corner and a mix of furniture including pew seats. Overlooking open countryside and the lake beyond the well-tended rear garden contains cut down tree trunk seating.

This well managed inn has a fine wine list and good range of real ales which presently include Wadworth 6X and their IPA, Butcombe Bitter plus guest ales.

An extensive home-made and freshly prepared menu is available every day 12–2 and 7–9, (9.30 Friday and Saturday). In addition to seasonal specialities, plough-man's and a Greek salad, the menu offers diners a selection of starters such as home-made soup, crispy wedges, egg mayonnaise, prawn cocktail and deep fried mushrooms followed by traditional favourites like home-made steak & kidney pie, meat lasagne, bangers, eggs, chips and beans and ham, eggs, chips and peas. There is a choice of grills, butterfly chicken breast, Barnsley chops, fish dishes and a vegetarian selection, which includes vegetable lasagne, balti vegetables, a crispy vegetable combo and home-made vegetable bake. Sunday lunchtimes the inn serves a choice of six traditional roasts. The dessert menu ranges from traditional home-made bread and butter pudding and treacle sponge to Blagdon banana boat and a rather naughty knickerbocker glory!

Weekday opening times 11–2.30 & 7–11. Sunday 12–3 & 7–10.30

Children welcome but dogs only in non-dining areas and patio.

Telephone: (01761) 462475.

Walk No. 4

Village lies on the A368 between Weston-Super-Mare and Bath. Turn into Church Street opposite the Live & Let Live pub and continue down towards the reservoir. The New Inn is on the right in Park Lane

Approximate distance: 5¼ miles. OS Map 172 ST 503/588.

There is a large car park at the pub but you can leave your vehicle almost anywhere outside.

A fairly easy and enjoyable walk around the very scenic Blagdon Lake, utilising peaceful country lanes and attractive foot and field paths.

From the pub continue down the lane ultimately turning right at the road junction, cross the bridge and immediately join the signed footpath on the right. The attractive path follows the edge of the reservoir for about a mile. Upon reaching the stile climb over and turn right, over the bridge and cross the stile on the right to re-join the path. Cross the next stile maintaining direction across the field to the gap then to the wooden crossing point keeping close to the hedge on the left. Cross the field and climb the stone stile turning left into the lane at West Town.

Take the next right following this high hedged peaceful lane until you reach a stile on the right then bear left down across the field towards the dwellings. Look for the stile on the left then carefully descend the steps turning right into Chapel Lane where you have good glimpses of the lake. Turn right at the next junction walking downhill then left into the driveway of Rugmoor Farm. In a few steps pass through the gate on the left, turn right and go through the farm gate, negogiate the stiles ahead bear left, up and across to more stiles, enter the field and walk down to the stiles in the bottom left-hand corner. Keeping close to the hedge continue down until you reach a wooden walkway into the field on the left, then bear right and make for the far corner, climb the stile into the lane and turn left.

Bear right at the next junction then join the signed footpath into the field on the right. Keeping close to the hedge descend to

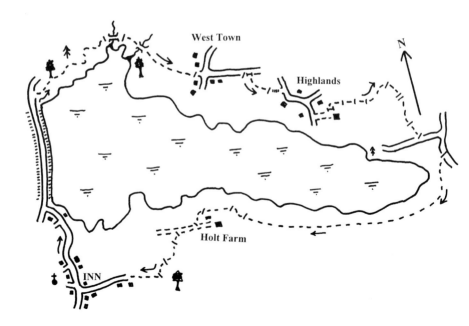

16

the stile maintaining direction to another stile and join the narrow path. From this point the route is well signed and easy to follow with a series of stiles before reaching Holt Farm. Stay in the field walking to the right, all the way round the farm, over the stile then straight ahead across to the stile, exiting onto the farm road. Turn right and in a short distance look for the stiles on the left, cross into the field and turn left. Keeping close to the hedge boundary, climb the field then cross the stile, go up the narrow path to the stile at the top and turn right following the path out into the lane turning right back to the pub.

The White Lion, Blagdon Hill

Lovingly refurbished the White Lion at Blagdon fits perfectly with its delightful surroundings. Built in the 1600's this very atmospheric and popular pub has two rooms divided by an ancient part plaster and beamed wall. The main bar is dominated by a large inglenook fireplace where a warm wood burning stove is lit on all but the warmest of days. Displayed all around are interesting antique copper and brass items whilst cartoon prints hang on the walls. There is a comfortable wooden chair by the fire, various wooden settles, tables and chairs. Summer imbibers can sit in the beer garden at the front.

The pub is a freehouse very efficiently run by the new owners Brian and Becky Hinton. Well-conditioned real ales presently available include Bass and Old Speckled Hen plus a local guest ale.

Available everyday of the week 12–2.30 and 7–9.30 freshly prepared dishes include baked mussels with onion, tomato, garlic and cheese, and a warm salad of calves liver, bacon, mushroom and onion relish. There is a choice of steaks, leg of lamb, breast of corn fed chicken stuffed with crab, mild mustard and brandy cream, breast of pigeon pan fried with plum and mustard and fillet of wild boar. Fish dishes, subject to availability, range from trout fillets poached in cider with basil and sole fillets with lobster, mussels, prawns and white wine sauce to sea bass poached with fennel, white wine, cream and prawns and scallops wrapped in bacon and grilled with lemon, garlic butter served on saffron rice plus six vegetarian dishes such as mushroom stroganoff and broccoli Stilton bake. Traditional bar snacks on offer include ploughman's, jacket potatoes, bacon, sausage, fried egg, tomato and saute potatoes, steak and kidney pie and grilled Cumberland sausage and mash.

Families are welcome and only well controlled dogs.

Opening times 12–3 & 7–11. (10.30 Sunday).

Telephone: (01823) 421296.

18

Leave the M5 at junction 26 and follow the sign for Ruggin, Lowton and Howleigh turning right at Blagdon Hill.

Approximate distance: 4¼ miles. OS Map 193 ST 211/182.

Large car park plus limited space on the opposite side of the road.

A paradise for wild flower lovers this extremely enjoyable but slightly demanding walk takes you first along an attractive country lane then up a pretty path through bluebell woods and across farm land to the road. The second half of the walk is even more attractive following woodland paths through broadleaf and conifer plantations and follows a very attractive stream leading to Curdleigh. The best time and perhaps only time is to walk from mid April onwards when the springtime display of wildflowers is stunning.

From the pub turn right, cross the road and climb the stile into the field following the path to the stile on the far side. Turn left into the lane then next right. Numerous spring flowers such as primroses, violets, bluebells, yellow archangel, pearlwort, and garlic smelling ransoms compete for all available hedgerow space. At the top of the lane keep straight ahead between the buildings and through the gate to join the grass track passing beyond. After a second gate this very attractive but somewhat stony track, carpeted with garlic ransoms rises steadily beside a pretty stream through bluebell woods then narrows further on and becomes a little uneven and wet especially at one point where a stream crosses.

Leave by the small gate following the path behind the hill, past an attractive bluebell wood on the right shortly to bear left through the metal farm gate. Bear left up to a similar gate, onto the track then turn right through the gate, through Priors Park Farm and out-buildings, up to the road and turn left.

In about a quarter of a mile, after passing Holybush Park Caravan Park, take the next track on the left leading to the stile and keep to the main track forking right through a mature conifer wood. Wide at first the track soon narrows then twists and turns descending through the trees eventually reaching a stream at the bottom (Look for a waymark on the tree on the left). Cross over and

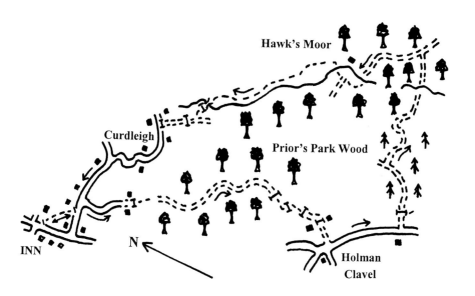

Walk No. 5

follow the grass path up to a similar cross path turning left.

This very attractive grass path descends through a deciduous wood where one can see more interesting wild flowers including violets and early purple spotted orchids. At the bottom cross the stream and bear right. The path rises up around the pumping station, bears right after passing the entrance gates then follows the stream into the woods. Keep walking along the well-trodden path until you reach a dense area of trees at which point bear left. (With careful observation you will see a waymark arrow on one of the trees). Walk down towards the stream following the waymark arrows nailed to trees at intervals along the route. Keep close to the stream eventually reaching the gate, cross the bridge, walk up to the track and turn right.

Pass through the gate and continue along the track, finally through one last gate turning left into the lane at Curdleigh. More attractive wild flowers fill the hedgerows including the bright blue forgetmenot. Ignore the footpath on the right but continue walking until you reach the stile on the right retracing your steps back across the field to the pub.

The Crown Inn, The Batch, Churchill

Rising abruptly out of the Sedgemoor Levels, the limestone Mendip Hills mark the northern boundary of the District. Churchill lies beneath the great prehistoric camp of Dolebury upon Mendip.

Peacefully located away from the main roads at the junction of a narrow lane and gravel track lies this timeless gem of a pub - a rare find today. Built from local stone it was originally an old coaching stop and once housed the village grocer's and butcher's shop. Built on a hillside each area is on a slightly higher level than the next. The small room on the left has a large fire and there are two more simply furnished seating areas, another fire and some pew seats on a slate floor. The bar on the right is larger, has cross beams and still retains its lovely original flagstone floor. There is a padded window seat, beer barrel for a table and a lovely raised fireplace in a large stone hearth behind which, up two steps, is a very cosy dining room overlooking the sheltered rear lawn with more tables at the front. Mendip Morris Men occasionally dance here.

The inn is a freehouse enthusiastically run by Tim Rogers offering a constantly changing list of real ales tapped straight from barrels at the back. These might include Batch Bitter brewed especially by Cotleigh, Smiles Golden Brew, Butcombe Bitter and Draught Bass.

Food is served at lunchtime only 12–2 and consists of snacks such as rare beef sandwiches, assorted salads, home-made soups, ploughmans and jacket potatoes plus specials like savoury crepes, cauliflower cheese with bread, prawn and avocado salad, home-made Stilton and pepper quiche. Treacle sponge and hot chocolate fudge cake feature on the pudding menu.

Children are allowed away from the bar and dogs on a lead in front garden.

Opening times 12–2.30 & 7–11.

Telephone: (01934) 852995.

Walk No. 6

Churchill lies on the A368 at its junction with the A38. Either turn off the A38 directly into Skinners Lane, or off the A368 at the Nelson Arms.

Approximate distance: 3 miles. OS Map 172 ST 448/598.

Parking in the lane is very limited at busy times additional parking is provided by the owner in the field opposite.

An extremely enjoyable, scenic walk high up onto Dolebury Warren and hill fort. The paths are generally good underfoot, well marked and easy to follow and although steep in some places not over demanding.

Leaving the front of the pub, turn right and right again into Skinners Lane, cross the main road to the kissing gate and join the path signposted, Burrington. Leave by the next kissing gate and bear left across the field to the metal steps in the corner turning right onto the footpath. Narrow in places and often slippery when wet the attractive path rises steadily towards a wood. Climb the fence and keep straight ahead through the trees then cross the track, pass through the gate, past the dwellings and cross the stile by the gate turning right.

This wide grass and stony track snakes its way up through bluebell woods quite steeply in places. Fork right at the path junction and, upon reaching the stile enter the field maintaining direction across to the stile beside the gate on the far side taking time to look back and enjoy the view. Keeping close to the boundary on the left reach the stile,

cross into the field and turn immediately right, cross a second stile following the well trodden path uphill then make a right at the fingerpost joining the Limestone Link. Turn left at the next fingerpost, pass through the trees and maintain direction to the stile and top of the fort. In summer the area is carpeted with attractive wild flowers including many blue harebells, pyramidal orchids, kidney vetch and yellow wort attracting butterflies like the small blue and grizzled skipper.

Leave the fort on the far side and keep walking in the same direction until reaching the trees at which point turn left and join the stony path down through the trees to the gate. Turn right, walk past the cottages, carefully cross the main road and head up the signed bridleway opposite turning right at the top down the gravel track to the pub.

22

View from the Fort

Wheatsheaf, Combe Hay

Close to Bath on the edge of a steep wooded valley this friendly old coaching inn is set high above the immaculately kept terraced gardens overlooking Cam Brook. Dovecotes are set into the white-painted stone front wall. The old fashioned rooms have low ceilings and an assortment of furnishings including high curved-back wooden settles. One of the smaller rooms has an attractive stone fireplace. There are lots of regalia on the walls together with stuffed birds and early photographs of the pub.

The inn is a freehouse still serving real ale traditionally straight from the cask, which presently includes Old Speckled Hen or Butcombe Bitter.

Excellent food is available everyday 12–2 and 6.30–9.30 (7 Sunday). On my visit the blackboard menu listed snacks of ploughman's and home-made soup followed by dishes such as smoked chicken and ham terrine, sweet and sour chicken and chicken breast in a marinade of smoked garlic, tarragon and olive oil served with a chasseur sauce. Also chalked up was pan-fried chicken livers with smoked bacon and warm vinaigrette and roast rack of lamb. Fish dishes included, sauted tiger prawns cooked in garlic butter, locally caught fillet of trout with a white wine, cream and dill sauce, escalope of salmon topped with basil and prawns wrapped in puff pastry and served with a white wine, Vermouth, saffron, tomato and cream sauce. The game special might be breast of pigeon filled with raspberries, wrapped in bacon and served with a rosemary, mint and red wine sauce, Vegetarians have a choice of meals like creamy wild mushrooms and pepper tagliatelle and deep fried brie coated with apricots, almonds and Cumberland sauce. Sweets range from home-made cheese cake to treacle sponge pudding.

Weekday opening times 11–2.30 & 6–10.30–(11 Friday & Saturday). Sunday 12–3 & 7–10.30.

Children in dining area, dogs allowed if well behaved.

Accommodation in three en-suite rooms. Also very good B&B at Anchor Farm $\frac{1}{4}$ mile up the lane towards Bath.

Telephone: (01225) 833504.

Village signed from the B3110 at Midford south of Bath.

Approximate distance: $2\frac{1}{2}$ miles. OS Map 172 ST 735/601.

There is ample parking at the pub but only limited space in the village.

A short scenic walk which follows a bridleway uphill beside a bluebell wood then dips down a rather wet and uneven track. After crossing the lane an attractive footpath climbs steadily beside the derelict Somerset Coal Canal then heads steeply up through a beech wood after which a field path rises to a track beginning the descent to the village.

Leave the pub turning right and then immediately left onto the signed bridleway. Follow this often muddy track up to the gate, into the field and straight ahead to the gate opposite. Climb the track ahead, up past the bluebell wood and through the small gate into the field. Walk all the way round the perimeter to the gate and turn left down the wide gravel track.

Before reaching the gateway turn left onto the narrow track. Steep, very uneven in places and often running with water it eventually levels before reaching a bridge. After crossing the river climb the stile on the left and join the path, which passes between farm buildings and rises to a stile.

Cross the road, go under the bridge and straight ahead to the gate. The path ahead rises past the old Somerset Coal Canal. Coal mining is one of Somerset's oldest industries and this canal was conceived as a quick and economical way of transporting coal from the north of the coal fields to Bath and further to the east. It received the Royal accent on the 17 April 1794 but closed soon after. As you follow the path you can still see many of the old lock gates.

Upon reaching the metal gate turn left over the plank bridge and follow the path which rises steeply up through the trees to a stile. Turn right and walk up the field to the stile at the top then left onto the track, down past the dwellings to the lane turning right back to the pub.

The Crown Inn, Creech Heathfield

Hard to imagine but the track in front of this old coaching inn was once the main route between Taunton and Bridgwater. Today this lovely thatched unpretentious inn is peacefully located away from the main road at the end of a short lane. It is deservedly popular with the locals who often refer to it as the Drum and Monkey. The main cosy bar is simply furnished, has bare stone walls and a large inglenook fireplace with winter log fire. There is a separate public bar, a skittle alley and attractive front beer garden.

The welcoming freehouse is personally run by the new owners Mark & Emma Pavey. Real ales presently available include Theakston Best and Butcombe Bitter.

Good home-cooked food is available every day 12–1.30 and 7–9.30. Apart from daily specials such as marinated chicken breasts, ploughman's, winter curries and summer salads the menu lists snacks of jacket potatoes, baguettes, garlic mushrooms on ciabatta bread and breaded lobster tails served with a garlic mayonnaise dip. Heading the list of meat dishes is a 10oz sirloin steak, gammon served with pineapple and melted cheese, beef lasagne, chilli with basmati rice, cottage pie and a Yorkshire pudding filled with roast beef, new potatoes, vegetables and gravy. Fish dishes range from breaded cod and scampi and chips to moules mariniere and butterfly king prawns whilst vegetarian dishes contrast between cauliflower cheese and Mexican bean casserole.

Weekday opening times 11.30–3 & 5–11. Saturday 11.30–3 & 5.30–11. Sunday 12–3 & 7–10.30.

Children and dogs equally welcome.

An extension is planned in the next few months when accommodation will be available.

Telephone: (01823) 412444.

The Inn is signed east from the main village street approached up Crown Lane.

Approximate distance: $2\frac{1}{2}$ miles OS Map 193 ST 280/272.

Ample parking at the pub and outside in the lane.

A short but very enjoyable walk which guides you first on field paths and tracks to reach the Bridgwater and Taunton Canal, one of few in the county still used today. After following the tow path the return route is along a peaceful country lane passing Charlton Orchards.

Leave the pub turning left and walk for a short distance along the track, originally the old coaching route. Bear right past the houses, turning right into the road then immediately left, past the dwelling to join the footpath on the right, which leads to a track running to the right. Continue ahead to the stile, cross into the field maintaining direction until you reach the track. Climb the stile in front of you and make for the stile opposite then bear right up the track to the road.

Turn left and follow this twisting track until you reach a small path on the left behind the dwelling. Re-join the track and continue walking towards the bridge, cross over and turn left through the gate along the attractive canal side path. Of the few Somerset canals that were built during the Industrial Revolution the Bridgwater to Taunton Canal was the only one to survive intact.

Amble for a mile then cross the bridge at Charlton bearing right then left. On the right is Charlton Orchards which is well worth a visit. They grow 23 varieties of apples plus, pears, plums, damsons and soft fruits in season. Open all year Monday –

Friday 10–6, Saturday 10–5 and Sunday 2–5. Simply keep to the lane, past the new golf course walking until you reach the track on the right then re-trace your steps back to the pub.

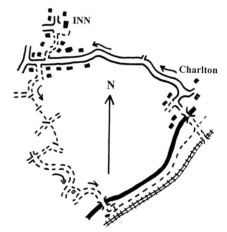

Walk No. 8

The New Inn, Dowlish Wake

There are two very good reasons to visit the picturesque village of Dowlish Wake, Perry's Cider Mill close to the ancient packhorse bridge and the lovely New Inn. Very popular with diners this excellent pub is one of my favourites. Draped with hops the warm and cosy main bar has a low beamed ceiling, a large open fireplace containing a single high back wooden settle with more high back settles around the walls. A flag-stoned corridor leads through to the skittle alley and small family room which overlooks the rear garden and play area. The dark beamed 'locals bar' has a warm wood burning stove, wall bench seating, pool table and table skittles.

The inn is a freehouse very well run by the owners David Small and Therese Boosey. Real ales presently available include Wadworth 6X, Butcombe Bitter and Theakston Old Peculier.

Very good reasonably priced English and Continental fayre, all home-made, can be enjoyed all week 12–2 and 7–9. Sunday 12–2 and 7–9 (summer only). Bar snacks on the menu (which include several children's/small meals) lists home-made soup, soft herring roes on toast, assorted sandwiches, ploughman's, salads and omelettes. Main meals listed include an all day breakfast, emince of liver with onions, bacon, mushrooms in a wine sauce, nut and lentil roast, pan fried fillet of sole, scampi tails, delicious cut ham with two eggs and chips, the famous bellew sausages served with rosti and salad garnish and various grills. There are a few specials on the blackboard like Somerset chicken, fish bake, lamb casserole and farmhouse pie plus a more comprehensive menu which offers a range of starters like herring fillet marinated with herbs and served with a garlic vinaigrette, followed by monkey gland – fillet steak stuffed with Stilton, served with a wine, mushroom and mustard sauce and Mediterranean vegetable and cheese welling-ton. Swiss specialities are cooked at the table. Sweet lovers will not be disap-pointed with raspberries in port jelly, spotted dick with custard and apple and blackberry pancakes.

Weekday opening times 11–3 & 6–11. Sunday 12–3 & 7–10.30.

Families and dogs welcome.

Telephone: (01460) 52413.

Walk No. 9

Village signed south of Ilminster.

Approximate distance: 4 miles. OS Map 193 ST 375/125.

Park in the road or the inn's own car park opposite.

An interesting an easy going ramble along peaceful country lanes and field paths guiding you through the pretty hamlets of Cricket Malherbie and Oxenford finally passing Perry's Cider Mills with its interesting museum. An ideal walk for all members of the family.

Go out of the pub turning right, walk up to the junction and pass through the gate into the field ahead (footpath signed Cudworth 1¼). Keeping close to the hedge on the right walk until you reach the gate then pass through into the field on the right, turn left and continue beside the hedge on your left. Further on pass through the hedge gap, negotiate the plank bridge (removable wire fences) and continue ahead, through a similar gap then cross a stile maintaining your direction through several gates following the rising grass track to Bonners Leaze Farm.

Bear left between the barn and dwellings, go up past the cottages and immediately cross the stile into the field on the right. Keep straight ahead through the gate finally leaving by the gate into the lane. Keep straight ahead turning right at the crossroads towards the pretty hamlet of Cricket Malherbie. After passing Cricket Court and the pretty church of Mary Magdelene, turn right at the next crossroads and follow the lane down, across the stream and up through the hamlet of Oxenford then take the next left into Moolham Lane.

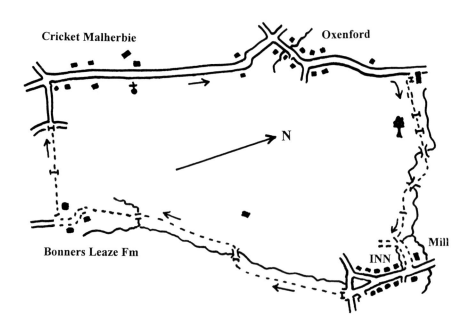

30

Walk as far as the dwelling at the bottom of the lane, the footpath is on the right. (The present footpath sign is just visible above the top of the hedge). A footpath diversion order was issued in February 1997 which will provide a stile south of the garden and should be well signed when or if the order goes through. Until the diversion is in place go through the small white gate, pass directly in front of the dwelling and make for the plank bridge in the boundary hedge. Go straight across the field to the gate, through the small bluebell wood and out by the gate opposite. Bear left down the field to the bridge and cross the stile into the field. The path arcs right towards a concrete bridge. Having crossed in to the field bear left to the stile, keep straight ahead to the gate and continue ahead close to the stream making for the dwelling and the stile.

The track passes Perry's Cider Mills and Museum well worth a visit. The Mill is open all year from 9–1 & 1.30–5.30 weekdays, Saturdays 9.30–1 & 1.30–4.30. Sunday 10–1. Turn right then fork left back to the pub.

The Horse & Groom, East Woodlands

Located in a lovely rural position and known locally as "The Jockey" this lovely two-storey, white washed stone country inn was built in 1677 as a small holding and only became a pub in 1785. Lots of light wood is evident in the small cosy lounge which has comfortable armchairs ideally positioned in front of the large open fireplace and wood burning stove providing ideal relaxation. A cosy feeling pervades in the opposite bar secluded from the doorway by a high back wooden settle. Features include the old flag-stoned floor and open log fire. An attractive addition is the side conservatory for family dining there is also a good-sized side garden and picnic benches at the front.

The pub is a freehouse very well run by the proprietors Tim & Ann-Marie Gould. Real ale is still served traditionally straight from the barrel and presently includes Butcombe Bitter, Wadworth 6X and Green King IPA plus a guest.

Bar food is available, Tuesday to Sunday 12–2 and Tuesday to Saturday 6.30–9. The menu might list snacks such as filled baguettes, ploughman's, home-made soup, salads, game pate, liver, bacon and onions in a rich gravy, ribeye steak with a red wine and mushroom sauce, pork escallope with Tewkesbury mustard in an asparagus sauce also smoked salmon salad and haddock and prawn casserole. Vegetarian dishes might include broccoli, leek and pecan nut bake and shell pasta cabonara, Sweets range from home-made summer pudding to caramelised rice pudding. At weekends a special menu is available. Starters range from warm toasted Somerset goats cheese served on a bed of baby spinach to crab and sweetcorn chowder, followed by roast Barbary duck breast sliced and served with apricot brandy sauce and fried medallions of beef fillet served with morel mushrooms and Madeira sauce and to finish sweets such as walnut betty – an individual sweet with layers of oats, caramel, banana, walnuts and baked till golden

Dogs on a lead, children under 14 not in the bar.

Opening times 11.30–2.30 & 6.30–11. Sunday 12–3 & 7–10.30.

No accommodation at pub but available opposite.

Telephone: (01373) 462802.

Village signed off the A361 south of Frome.

Approximate distance: 5 miles. OS Map 183 ST 792/446.

Park where you can at the front.

A series of field paths and tracks guide you through the hamlets of Elliots Green, Blatchbridge and West Woodlands. The walk, best suited for the fitter members of the family twice crosses the River Frome and passes a short way through an attractive bluebell wood. The last time I was here the paths were badly marked and the majority of crossing points no more than parallel planks, progress can be slow but I am assured the situation will improve.

Leave the pub and walk down the lane opposite, past the dwellings then cross the stile into the field on the left. Bearing right climb the stile in the far hedge and maintain direction to a similar stile and cross one more field following the narrow and often overgrown path through the small plantation to the stile. Bear right up to the gate, round the farmyard, out into the lane and turn left.

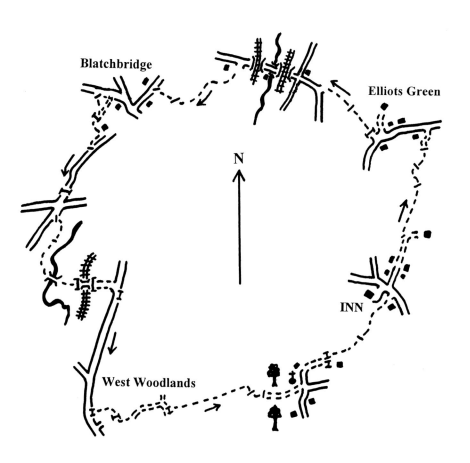

33

Walk No. 10

Upon reaching Elliots Green turn onto the gravel track leading to Elm Tree Cottage and almost immediately pass through the gate into the field on the left. Go over the wooden crossing point and carry on beside the hedge, over another crossing point and out into the lane. Walk straight ahead, carefully crossing the by-pass, go under both railway bridges then turn immediately left along the track and into the field. Bearing right walk up to the stile in the hedge maintaining direction to another then bear left across a pair of stiles, turn right up to another stile and walk to the gap in the top hedge, out into the lane and turn left.

Turn right at the main B3092 and keeping to the right-hand side, walk a short distance then cross over into the lane on the left. Fairly soon cross the stile into the small field on the left and bear left down to the far corner. Go through the gate into the field, keep straight ahead to the stile in the bottom hedge, make your way down towards the dwelling, round the hedge to the stile, out into the lane and turn right. Carefully cross the by-pass and almost immediately climb the stile into the field on the left. Bearing half right make your way over to the crossing points and plank bridge then follow the river bank up to another crossing point (when I was last here no more then a broken gate). Walk beside the hedge then go left through the gap and gate into the field keeping straight ahead to the gate in the left-hand corner. Pass over the attractive stone bridge following the path up the rise to the gate ahead of you, cross the railway bridge to the gate, go up the track to the road and turn right.

There is a footpath opposite, clearly marked on the OS Map leading to East Woodlands but was not signed or evident during my visit to the area. I am assured the local authority will get round to it eventually but until this happens of if you prefer a slightly longer walk turn right along the road. Upon reaching West Woodlands turn left through the gate close to the horse chestnut tree (it is almost opposite a recently restored farm cottage). Walk up the field arcing right, go through the gate and turn left along the track, through the farm, over the bridge and onto the track ahead. Turn right at the top then pass through the gate nearest to the pylon. Walk straight ahead up to the crossing point in the far hedge. As there is a wire fence beside the ditch bear right, go left through the gateway and half left up to the crossing point in the top hedge. Bear right to the crossing point in the top corner, turn left up the field, cross into the bluebell wood and walk to the church at the top.

Turn left into the lane, past the dwellings then bear right up the drive, through the small wooden gate and along the path to the stile. Cross the field to the stile and join the pretty path down to the lane and back to the pub.

The Inn at Freshford, Freshford

Occupying a glorious riverside setting this lovely old, three-storey stone building, bedecked in hanging baskets is a welcoming site on a summer's day. An
interesting feature at the front is the stone staircase leading to upstairs rooms.
On the right-hand side of the linked bars is a large stone fireplace with open
winter fire behind which a couple steps lead to a small dining area. For summer
imbibers there is an attractive terraced rear beer garden.

Once owned by Ushers then part of the Inntrepreneur Pub Group the inn is
now part of Scottish Courage. Three regularly changing real ales might include
Draught Bass, Marston's Pedigree and Smiles Best.

Nicely presented and well portioned food is available every day 12–2 and 6–10
(7 Sunday). Apart from chef's specials such as halibut fillet with a citrus sauce,
a trio of sausages – wild boar, venison and Cumberland, the Inn steak sandwich
served topped with fried onions and melon and prawn salad, the set menu lists
chef's soup, deep fried brie, avocado and goats cheese, Stilton mushrooms and
smoked trout terrine followed by steaks and grills. Also listed on the menu is a
mini leg of lamb, slow roasted and served with a redcurrant and rosemary sauce,
half a smoked chicken, venison steak, medallions of beef, pan fried and served
with a red wine and Roquefort sauce, duck breast cooked pink and served with
an orange and Cointreau sauce, roasted Stilton pork steak, butterflied with a rich
creamy Stilton cheese sauce and Somerset chicken supreme stuffed with Stilton
wrapped in bacon and served with a white wine sauce. Traditional favourites
include ham, egg and chips, steak and ale pie and home-made lasagne. For
vegetarians there is a broccoli bake, home-made vegetarian lasagne and spinach
& feta cheese parcels. There are of course the usual snacks of assorted ploughman's, sandwiches and baked potatoes plus a children's menu. Desserts range
from home-made banoffee pie, spotted dick and treacle sponge to strawberry
pavlova and Marshfield real dairy ice cream.

Weekday opening times 11–3 & 6–11 Sunday 12–3 & 7–10.30.
Children and dogs both equally welcome.
Telephone: (01225) 722250.

Walk No. 11

Village signed from the A36 south of Bath. Pub at the eastern end of the village close to the river.

Approximate distance: 2 miles. OS Map 172 ST 792/600.

Plenty of parking at the pub plus ample space in the road at the front.

A short but very enjoyable family stroll affording scenic views over the village to the fields beyond. Perfect for a Sunday morning, the walk follows field and woodland paths and although some are steep and a little demanding they are generally good underfoot.

Leave the pub turning right, cross the bridge, walk to the bend and climb the stile into the field on the right. Follow the path across both fields to the stile and turn right into the lane. Walk round, over the bridge and up the lane until you reach the signed bridleway on the left.

Walk round in front of the dwelling and up the gravel track leading to the woods. The path rises steadily beside mature woodland carpeted with garlic ransoms, some bluebells and many other wild flowers. Upon reaching the stile enter the field and bear right walking up beside the fence until you come to the kissing gate on the right then pass through onto the track. There is a nice

bluebell wood on the left but many other wild flowers can be seen including primroses, mullion and yet more ransoms. Go through the gate and across the field to the kissing gate opposite, up the path to the lane and turn left.

Further up the hill take the signed path on the right, which enters a field, follows the boundary to a kissing gate in the far corner then descends to the road. Turn right and just past the War Memorial take the stepped grass path on the right, which runs beside the trees to meet a wall on the far side. Turn right then fork left following the path through the trees down the hillside to the field turning left back to the pub.

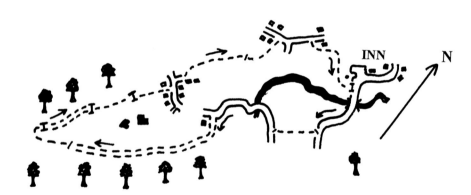

The Lord Poulett, Hinton St George

All the houses including the pub in this beautifully kept village, a past winner of "the best kept village in Somerset" competition, are built from local ham stone. Named after the Poulett family this atmospheric 17th century pub recently re-opened following refurbishment. The sunny front bar is divided by a central fireplace serving two rooms, which are carpeted and comfortably furnished with refectory and other tables, country chairs and high back pine settles. Paintings and various jugs decorate the walls and there is a second fireplace in the end stone wall housing a warm winter log fire. On the left of the entrance passage is a small dining room dominated by a massive step-in inglenook fireplace beside which are an enormous pair of bellows. The inn also has an attractive rear beer garden with boules pitch.

Owners of this freehouse Geoffrey and Lynn Bussell administer proceedings behind the bar presently dispensing four real ales directly from the barrel which include Butcombe Bitter, Otter Ale, Young's Special and a guest.

Very good home cooked food is available seven days a week 12–2 and 7–9.30. A roast is served at lunchtime on Sunday but no food in the evening. The interesting weekday menu lists starters such as a warm duck and mandarin salad and asparagus spears, pan fried with garlic and balsamic vinegar followed by dishes ranging from baked loin of rabbit stuffed with apple and pistachio nuts and collops of beef braised with caramelised onions and served in Butcombe ale to a medley of summer vegetables stroganoff in a cider and cream sauce, served with a timbale of rice. Brie and broccoli pithivier served with a light cheese sauce and risotto cakes made from rice and cumin with a tomato and cream cheese filling, breadcrumbed, deep fried and served with a tomato coulis are two variations on the á la carte menu. Expect to find ploughman's, sandwiches, salads and a fisherman's platter on the specials board.

Families welcome, dogs under supervision.

Opening times 12–2.30 & 7–11. (10.30 Sunday).

Telephone: (01460) 73149.

Walk No. 12

Village signed $1\frac{3}{4}$ miles north off the A30 west of Crewkerne.

Approximate distance: $5\frac{1}{4}$ miles. OS Map 193 ST 422/127.

Rear car park plus parking anywhere along the road at the front.

This fairly scenic walk, ideal for a sunny Sunday afternoon, follows field paths, tracks and established tree lined bridleways. Some parts can be muddy in winter better though in late spring which is a good time to see primroses.

Turn left from the pub, over the crossroads following the lane ahead until you reach the footpath on the left sign-posted, Edgewood $\frac{1}{2}$. Keep straight ahead across the field to the stile, over more stiles and through farm gates leaving by the gate into the lane. Walk to the tarred drive opposite signed, to the church. Upon reaching the lane turn left and go over the stile on the right following the little path behind the church, round to the stile then bear right across the small field to the stile opposite and turn left following the narrow path signed, to Wigborough. Turning right will bring you to the village of Merriott, which has some attractive cottages and well worth a glance. There is also a plant nursery in the village.

At the end of the path cross the stile then keep straight ahead down the field and up to the stile in the hedge crossing onto the bridleway then turn left. Often muddy underfoot this narrow track soon widens with a better surface. Walk up to the road and join the track opposite bearing left at the cross track and go out into the road. Cross over and join the narrow path opposite running uphill beside the hedge signed, Hinton St George. From this sandy, tree lined path there are good views north to the villages of Lopen, Over Stratton and Seavington St Michael.

Turn right into the lane and immediately join the footpath on the left signed, Summer Lane $\frac{1}{3}$ miles. Maintain direction along

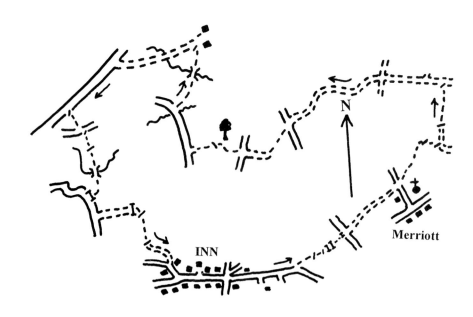

this ill-defined path which soon dips through a rather wet area of scrub. At the point where a small stream drains into the valley enter the small wooded area and follow the often overgrown path up the bank to the stile and straight ahead across the field to the stile in the furthest point in the far hedge. At the lane turn right. (Turning left will take you back to the pub).

After crossing the bridge take the footpath on the right signed, to Lopen. Enter the field bearing half left and make your way across to the bridge in the far hedge. Go into the field on the left and bear right up to the crossing point by the farm buildings then turn left along the track, finally climbing the

crossing point into the road.

Turn left, and when you reach the stile on the left, cross the field turning left into Summer Lane shortly to climb the stile into the field on the right. Cross to the next stile and keep straight ahead to the bridge, which spans an attractive tributary of Lopen Brook. Climb the steps to the stile and make for the gate opposite, turn left into the lane then left again along the track. Pass through the gate, cross the stile into the field on the right and climb to the stile at the top. The very attractive path rises steeply up to the road emerging opposite the church at which point turn left back through this very pretty village to the pub.

Key to Symbols

══════ road	---------- track	---------- undefined path
✔ stile	⟩══⟨ bridge	├──┤ gate
┤ ├ gap in hedge	⊟ cattle grid	

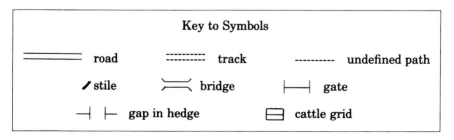

The sketch maps in this book are not necessarily to scale but have been drawn to show the maximum amount of detail.

The Old Inn, Holton

Originally a 400 year old coaching inn The Old Inn is today a popular and welcoming village local. The one main, atmospheric beamed bar, dominated by a large open stone fireplace with wood burner, has part wood panelled walls with lots of old copper and brass items. A nice mix of tables chairs and stools are positioned on both sides of the original flag-stoned floor. There is a piano, a large collection of key fobs on the ceiling by the bar and dressed sticks for sale displayed in large brass cartridge cases. A very attractive cosy stone-walled dining room seats up to 20 people. A hatch in the hallway serves both the small flower-filled front terrace and the raised rear beer garden, which has picnic benches and children's play area.

The inn is a freehouse owned and well run by Lin and Lou Lupton, There are two real ales generally available, Butcombe Bitter and Wadworth 6X plus a guest such as Otter Ale.

Bar food is available everyday 12–2 and 7–10 (except Sunday evening) together with an á la carte menu and a Sunday roast, pre-booking only. Blackboard specials such as garlic bread, deep fried whitebait, hot cheese and onion baguette, butterfly prawns with garlic mayonnaise and Oriental king prawns in filo pastry with a sweet and sour sauce might supplement the bar menu which lists a good range of snacks. The present choice is between home-made soup of the day, sandwiches and ploughman's also a mixed grill, various steaks, sherried beef and mushroom vol-au-vent, ham and eggs, lasagne and a pork curry. The more comprehensive restaurant menu lists sole 'St. Agnes' – grilled fillets of sole with crunchy breadcrumb topping and sliced chicken breast with Stilton and cider. There is a children's selection and tempting sweets like fruit filled pancakes flamed in brandy.

Weekday opening times 12.30–3 & 6–11. Saturday 12–11. Sunday 12–3 & 7–10.30.

Dogs on leads in bar only. Children 14 and above in bar, slightly younger if dining with parents.

Telephone: (01963) 32002.

Village located just south of Wincanton between the A303 and A357.

Approximate distance: 2½ miles. OS Map 183 ST 685/267.

There is a car park at the side plus limited space in the village.

A short but interesting scenic ramble across fields to ancient Maperton village whose Manor was recorded in the Domesday Book. It is said that traces of a castle and medieval village can still be seen in outlying fields. The going is generally easy underfoot ideal for all members of the family.

From the pub turn left and immediately join the public footpath opposite sign-posted, Maperton 1 mile. Keep straight ahead and pick up the grass path at the rear of the building leading to the metal gate. Cross to the stiles and maintain direction to the stone stile, over a couple more wooden stiles eventually leading to a large field at which point bear left up to the stile in the far top corner. Finally bear right up to the stone stile in the hedge, go out into the lane and turn right.

Turn left in the centre of the village then next left towards Charlton Harethorne. Carry on along the lane, down the dip and pass through the metal gate into the field on the left footpath sign-posted, to Hooke Lane ¾ mile. Keep to the hedge on the left, pass through the gate and go up the field, through the gate maintaining direction beside the hedge. Finally leave by the gate at the top and turn right into the lane.

Turn right, walk for awhile then take the lane on the left signed, to Holton ½. (If you wish to avoid walking all the way back along the lanes there is a track on the left which joins the path from the village). At the road junction turn left up past the 14th century church of St Nicholas forking left back to the pub

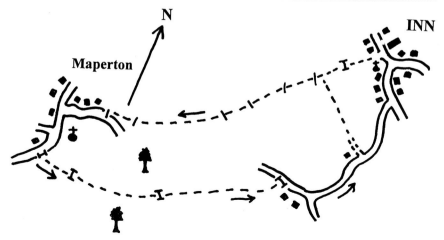

41

Kingsdon Inn, Kingsdon

The village of Kingsdon is amongst the prettiest in Somerset with many beautifully kept cottages and gardens so it was no disappointment when I arrived for the first time at the Kingsdon Inn. This very pretty thatched pub has a cottage garden feel about it especially as the path leads straight up the front garden to the door. Either side of the stone entrance are two attractive cosy rooms both with low beamed ceilings, large open fireplaces and an assortment of solid scrubbed farmhouse tables and chairs. The bar is at the rear on a lower level with more seating by the fireplace.

Having recently taken over this freehouse Ann & Les Hood are maintaining the very high standard. Three real ales presently available include London Pride, Mendip Gold and Tawny Bitter.

Very popular with diners food is available all week 12–2 and 7–9.30, Sunday evening limited snack menu 7–9 includes soup, jacket potatoes and ploughman's. Starters range from soused herring with dill sauce and Greek salad with garlic bread followed by grilled salmon fillet with parsley butter, baked haddock and prawn mornay, gammon steak, chicken in cider, grilled lambs liver with bacon and onions, beef steak, kidney and mushroom pie with Guinness, ham egg and chips, venison sausages, walnut, leek and Stilton pie and Mediterranean flan. Additions to the evening menu include fish soup, Kingsdon hors'd'oeuvre plate and salads of smoked salmon and prawn, smoked chicken and fresh pineapple and grilled goats cheese. Main dishes include monkfish with a white wine and garlic sauce, pork tenderloin with apricots and almonds, wild rabbit in a Dijon sauce, half a roast duck in a scrumpy sauce, turkey escalopes in hazelnut and orange sauce, roast rack of lamb and wild mushroom strudel in a wild mushroom sauce. Mango cheesecake heads the pudding list followed by sticky ginger pudding, lemon sponge with lemon sauce and Turkish delight ice-cream.

Weekday opening times 11–3 & 6–11. Sunday 12–3 & 7–11.

Families welcome.

Telephone: (01935) 840543.

Village signed from the B3151 off the A372 north of Ilchester.

Approximate distance: 3½ miles.   OS Map 183 ST 521/263.

Park beside the inn or in the lane at the front.

An enjoyable scenic walk, not over demanding along peaceful tracks and attractive field paths to Charlton Mackrell returning through Kingsdon Wood. An ideal family walk for a summers day. Lytes Cary Manor, a short distance east of Kingsdon is a charming 14th-century manor house and chapel whilst the attractive hedged gardens are full of trees and plants typical of the 16th-century. Restored in this century by Sir Walter Jenner the property is now owned by The National Trust open to the public April–October: Monday, Wednesday and Saturday 2–6.

Go out from the inn turning right, straight ahead at the bend then next right opposite The Old Stores. Cross the road keeping straight ahead past the dwellings, over the gravel track and join the signed footpath ahead. This peaceful track descends beside woods down Nut Hill to a gate. Follow the grass track beyond across the field to the gate then bear slightly left making for the gap by the oak.

Organic farming persists on many farms in the area and when I was here in July it was a pleasure to walk across this particular field which was amass of wild flowers and butterflies. Cross the corner of the field to the concrete bridge following the track ahead up between the fields, over the bridge turning left into the lane at Charlton Mackrell.

In a very short time go over the stile into the field on the left and bear right on the well-beaten path to the small bridge. Cross into the field and turn left walking beside the hedge all the way to the top of the field, round to the stile, out onto the bridleway and turn left.

This attractive stone-surfaced track rises fairly steeply through Kingsdon Wood, which consists mostly of mature beech and coppiced hazel and is home to many wild flowers including bluebells. Follow the track out of the wood to the right, over the cross track and along the peaceful lane. Upon reaching the village turn left then left again past The Garden House nursery, a must for perennial lovers. Further on fork right then left at the end of the lane retracing your steps back to the inn

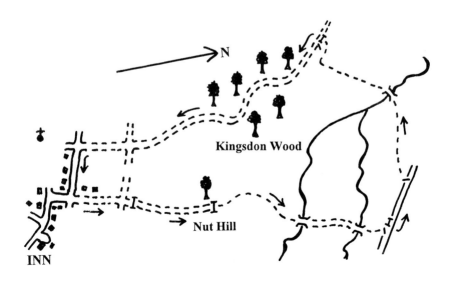

The Rising Sun Inn, Knapp

The Rising Sun is a delightful 15th century longhouse remotely situated amidst the beautiful Somerset Levels. The warm friendly atmosphere strikes you from the moment you enter and pervades throughout this lovely old inn. A deep chesterfield settee is perfectly placed to slump on a cold winter's night in front of the warm log-burning stove set in a massive inglenook fireplace. Past restoration has exposed ancient carved ceiling beams and a rustic wood screen separating an attractive beamed candlelit dining area. The old staircase can still be seen on the left of the fireplace. A similar attractive room on the opposite side of the entrance passage has bare stone walls and yet another inglenook fireplace with bread oven and range. During the summer one can sit on the sunny front terrace or on the small vine covered terrace at the back.

The inn is a freehouse extremely well run by the owner Tony Atkinson and his efficient staff. The well stocked bar includes an interesting wine list and two real ales presently Exmoor Ale and Draught Bass.

Excellent food is served at the inn resulting in numerous accolades. The menu available all week 12–2 and 7–9.30 is predominantly fresh fish from Brixham and St Mawes. There are lunchtime snacks such as open sandwiches, ploughman's, Welsh rarebit and ham, egg and saute potatoes with the main menu available in the evening. Heading the list is a very good gravadlax, bouillabaisse, crab and prawn gratin, smoked eel and seafood platter, prawn and avocado salad and moules marinere (small & large portions). To follow grilled Dover sole, John Dory served with sun dried tomatoes, anchovies and capers, scallops with mushrooms poached in a Vermouth, Dijon mustard and cream sauce, salmon with a creme fraiche and cucumber sauce, monkfish and salmon marinaded and skewered served on a bed of rice with a sherry sauce. There are two vegetarian options a nut roast with a Provencale sauce and a mushroom stroganoff, a reasonably priced Sunday roast and chef's specials.

Weekday opening times 11.30–2.30 & 6.30–11. Sunday 12–3 & 7–10.30.

Families welcome no dogs.

Overnight accommodation in two comfortable wooden chalets.

Tel/Fax: (01823) 490436.

Leave the A358 Southeast of Taunton and take the A378 Langport turning. Further on fork left sign-posted, North Curry and Stoke St Gregory. Soon after passing the North Curry sign turn left into the lane sign-posted Knapp and Creech, then simply follow the signs to the pub.

Approximate distance: $4\frac{1}{2}$ miles. OS Map 193ST 304/257.

Car park at the rear plus space in the lane at the front.

An interesting and scenic walk which explores West Sedge Moor, an area of the Somerset Levels. A path first crosses wetlands beside the River Tone, then Hay Moor before a steep attractive gully delivers you to the tiny hamlet of Moredon. Field paths then lead you to the ancient church of St Peter & Paul at North Curry before guiding you back to the pub. Apart from one steep section the walk is not demanding but can be very muddy in a few places during the winter. The Levels and Moors of Somerset are the most important areas of 'wetland' left in Southern England. Willow growing and basket making is one of the County's oldest industries and although once employing many hundreds of people is happily experiencing a revival.

Leave the pub turning right, down the lane to Haymoor End then turn left along the drove track (can be muddy). Turn right at the cross track, go over Knapp Bridge then through the gate on the right and follow the raised riverbank. Withy beds can be seen on the left of this area which is a large RSPB reserve and home to, lapwings, curlews, snipe and a few black tailed godwits which nest in the damp peat meadows. Also in

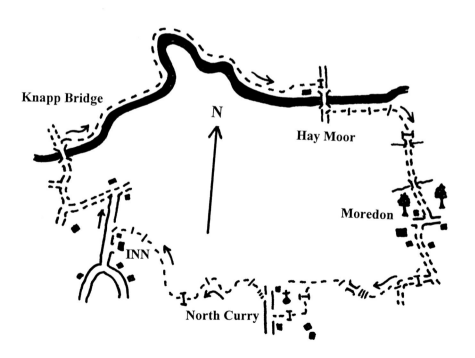

summer look out for the Southern aeshna dragonflies. After a series of gates and crossing points the path finally dips to the left past a dwelling leading to a gate which allows access to the road.

Turn right, over the bridge and climb the stile into the field on the left. Pass through three gates then bear right across the meadow towards the gate and bridge over the ditch and join the track beyond crossing Haymoor Old Rhyne. Keep straight ahead up the hillside. This very attractive water eroded gully, home to many harts tongue ferns, rises quite steeply to a stile near the top at Moredon. Pass in front of the dwelling and down the drive. After walking past a red brick dwelling on the left you will see a gate and stile on the right marked with the TDBC trail sign. Walk up this drive, round to the left and cross the stile into the field on the right. Follow the flattened track to the stiles and steps at the bottom of the field keeping straight ahead beside the hedge then up the bank on the left and through the kissing gate into the churchyard.

Built about 1300 it occupies the site of a Norman church of which only the north door remains. Once plastered the exterior, built from soft local quarried stone and golden ham stone is constantly being eroded and presents an ever-increasing problem. Inside you will notice stone seats around the base of the massive piers supporting the tower, a survival from pre-pew days, when churchgoers stood up, and 'the weakest went to the wall'.

From the front of the church continue walking west, pass through the kissing gate, down the path to the road and turn right. In a hundred or so paces climb the steps leading to the stile and enter the field on the left. Keeping near the hedge walk to the crossing point and continue ahead to the stile in the far hedge, bearing right walk over the brow of the field and down to the stile and plank bridge. Climb the field beside the hedge then cross the stile into the adjoining field. Follow the well signed path until you reach the gate, pass through and bear right across to the stiles in the hedge. Make your way ahead over to another stile keeping to the direction of the arrows, cross yet more stiles and a crossing point and after two more stiles turn left, walk down the field and leave by the stile at the bottom turning left back up to the pub.

Knapp Bridge

The Three Horseshoes, Langley Marsh

You will often see vintage cars on the forecourt of this unspoilt village local. Enthusiasts meet here on the 2nd Tuesday evening of each month for a 'natter n noggin' with the landlord John Hopkins himself an owner. Aptly the main bar, heated by a small open fire, is bedecked with motoring regalia including photographs and prints. Two model planes are suspended from the high area of the ceiling whilst numerous beer mats occupy the remaining wall space. A small cosier room is dominated by a large high back wooden settle whilst a large wooden refectory table and stick back chairs beside the open fire are the main features in a stone and panelled room at the front. There is a small attractive beer garden with children's play area and small front forecourt where Morris Men occasionally perform.

The pub is a freehouse enthusiastically run by the friendly owners at present serving three well-conditioned real ales, Palmer's IPA, Bitter and Fullers' London Pride.

Good imaginative food is served everyday 12–2 and 7–9.30. Daily specials like cheesy prawn and leek stuffed mushrooms, trout baked with tomatoes and cider, Algerian lamb, beef curry and leek and tomato pancakes supplement the printed menu which lists large ploughman's, salads and a choice of deep-pan home-made pizzas. Jacket potatoes come with a choice of ten fillings but if you prefer something different they will do their best. There is home-made thick vegetable and lentil soup a meal in itself, also garlic mushrooms and tuna stuffed tomatoes, followed by chilli, fish pie and steak and kidney pie cooked in ale. Vegetarians can choose between butter bean bourguignon and creamy vegetable and cheese bake. Children have their own menu. Favourite sweets include mincemeat, apple and brandy pancakes and spotted dick and custard.

Well behaved children in a restricted area, dogs outside on patio only.

Weekday opening times 12–2.30 & 7–1. Sunday 12–2.30 & 7–10.30. Closed all day Monday out of season.

Telephone: (01984) 623763.

Walk No. 16

Village signed from the B3227 (formerly the A361) at Wiveliscombe.

Approximate distance: 6 miles (2¼ miles). OS Map 181 ST 074/292.

Ample parking in road at front.

A fairly long but extremely enjoyable walk, (with a shorter option). After strolling through the village our walk takes you up a lovely old drove road then down a field to meet a pretty track eventually joining a path through Combe Bottom a large wooded vale leading to Brompton Ralph. After negotiating field and farm paths the walk continues along peaceful country lanes passing through Whitefield and Chorley's.

From the pub turn left down the hill walking to the bend at which point go up the little track on the left beside Sandycot Cottage. Narrow at first it soon widens into a very attractive cobble-surfaced gully where many wild flowers cling to the high steep-sided sandstone cliffs. At the track cross to the stile opposite and head down the field making for the stile at the bottom. Follow the path to a second stile and plank bridge then up the track ahead.

Although shared for part of the way with a small stream this delightful fern-lined track is generally good underfoot. Walk round until you reach the second stile on the right just this side of a narrow track. (For a short walk you continue following the track, out into the lane and straight ahead through the village of Whitefield then turn right on

the bend). Cross the field to the stile opposite, go over the plank bridge, up the path and turn left following the track into Combe Bottom.

Keep to this undulating forest path, which follows a line fairly close to the stream. Mostly coniferous the woods are home to many wild flowers including bluebells. Ignore the path across the stream but continue ahead on the wider track, which rises steadily beside a bluebell wood.

Turn left upon reaching the lane then left again at Brompton Ralph passing in front of the post office and join the lane on the left to Clatworthy. Walk up the hill turning left when you reach Westcott Farm sign-posted, to Bowden Farm 1 mile. Walk down to the farm buildings and go through the metal gate on the right, across the farmyard, past

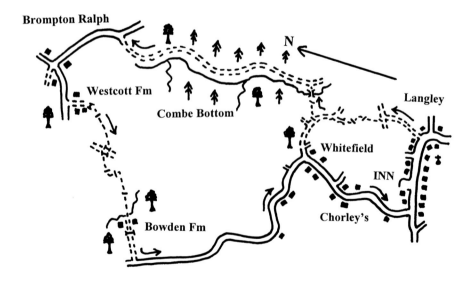

the dwelling and through the gate into the field. Keeping close to the hedge on the right walk to the metal gate on the far side and go over the track to the gate opposite. Stay close to the hedge behind the dwelling, make for the gate then turn immediately left, through the gate into the field and turn right. Keep close to the hedge across to the gate and into the field ahead. Go over the stream on the far side and up the fairly steep track until you eventually reach Bowden Farm. Pass through the yard, up the track to the lane and turn left.

Simply follow this very attractive, peaceful flower filled lane until you eventually reach the little village of Whitefield. When I was last here there were peacocks parading around a property on the right. Walk round the bend, past the dwellings and at the next bend (Whitefield Corner) turn right towards Chorley's. This lovely peaceful lane twice crosses a stream before reaching the village the pub is a short way down on the left.

Combe Bottom

The Royal Oak, Luxborough

Remotely hidden in the peaceful folds of the Brendon Hills lies a charming and totally unspoilt rural gem of immense character. Many accolades have been heaped on The Royal Oak over the years including CAMRA's 'Somerset Pub of the Year' in 1990 and Egon Ronay's award for 'Good Beer, Cider, Food and B&B'. Here time has stood still simple farmhouse tables, chairs and old pew settles are positioned on the flag-stone floor in front of the large open stone fireplace. Under a thatched roof, the rear bar which also has a flag-stone floor and nice open fireplace, is used by a local folk club on Friday nights. Three further rooms are all different in character, one has farmhouse seating, one has green decor with old mahogany furniture and the other is finished in red. There are a couple of picnic benches on the small front terrace with more on the lawn at the back.

Drinks in this freehouse are dispensed from a hatch in the wall. The real ales listed during my visit included Cotleigh Tawny, Exmoor Gold, Exmoor Stag, Juwards, Withy Cutter and Flowers IPA plus local ciders.

Food is available 12–2 and 7–10 (9.30 Sunday). Daily blackboard specials could include home-made cream of broccoli and Stilton soup, fresh monkfish, game pie, fillet steak with red wine and onion sauce and wild boar sausages with a Cumberland sauce. The set menu lists home-made pork and Stilton pate and garlic mushrooms served with onions in white wine followed by venison casserole, fillet of pork cooked with apple in a Calvados and cream sauce, chicken breast poached in brandy served with a ginger and cream sauce and lamb with apricots. Evening starters like smoked duck might precede salmon and sole fillets wrapped and cooked in filo pastry and served with a creamed tarragon and white wine sauce or a vegetarian curry. Sweets usually include bread and butter pudding.

Opening times 11–2.30 & 6–11. Sunday 12–2.30 & 7–11.

Children in one bar only, dogs welcome inside and out.

Excellent overnight accommodation in 10 en-suite rooms. Also at Pool Farm Byres in converted barn five minutes walk away.

Telephone: (01984) 640319.

Walk No. 17

Remotely situated Luxborough, which comprises the hamlets of Churchtown, Kingsbridge and Pooltown is best reached from the B3190 Watchet to Ralegh's Cross road but can also be reached from the A396.

Approximate distance: 3 miles. OS Map 181 SS 984/377.

Park in the lane or the large car park close by.

A fairly arduous but nevertheless very enjoyable scenic walk in the Brendon Hills at first up an attractive bridleway to Lower Court Farm and down through woodland to Druid's Combe. Wide undulating gravel tracks then guide you for some distance uphill through Slowley Wood before following the lane and short field path back to the pub.

From the pub cross the bridge, turn right and shortly turn left up the lane onto the bridleway sign-posted, to Lower Court Farm and Treborough. Follow this flower-lined track steeply uphill and join the pretty narrow path ahead. (Can be become overgrown in summer) Pass trough the gate and cross the field to the small gate opposite, go round to the left of the farm buildings and through the gate turning left onto the bridleway sign-posted, Druid's Combe and Luxborough.

Enter the field and walk round keeping to the hedge on the left then pass through the gate on the left (fingerpost on the right). Walk down the field beside the hedge on the

right, go through the gate and turn right. The track descends gently through coniferous woodland to reach the lane in the valley.

Keep straight ahead over the bridge and climb the narrow bridleway opposite signposted, to Slowley Wood. The path zigzags up the hillside, widens and then climbs steadily and steeply between tall conifer and broadleaf woodland, bearing left at the top and crossing an area of cascading water. Further on fork right and continue climbing through mixed woodland before descending a fair distance to a gate. Cross the stone bridge and turn right into the lane.

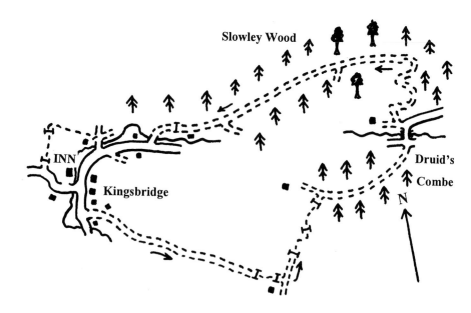

Carry on walking, past a dwelling on the right, turning right when you reach the lane sign-posted, to Withycombe. Walk up past the houses and cross the stile into the field on the left, keep straight ahead crossing the stream then climb to the gate and turn left. From the path ahead one has a very good view of the village which joins the lane leading down towards the pub.

Luxborough

Whatley Church

53

The Talbot Inn, Mells

The origins of the nursery rhyme 'Little Jack Horner' stem from this lovely village. According to legend Little Jack Horner was the steward to Richard Whiting Abbot of Glastonbury at the time of the Dissolution. In an attempt to make peace he sent to the king the deeds of 12 manors which belonged to Glastonbury hidden for safety in a large pie. Jack Horner was entrusted with the task and when safely out of sight slightly lifted the pastry crust and removed the deeds for the Manor of Mells. Although Jack Horner seems to be a fictional character Thomas Horner did in fact once own The Manor but relatives maintain that he bought it from the King.

This lovely old 15th century coaching inn has a cobbled entrance behind large wooden doors. A comfortable lounge and public bar lead off the attractive courtyard where there is lots of sheltered seating.

The inn is a freehouse offering a choice of two real ales Butcombe Bitter and Draught Bass.

The Talbot is a popular place to eat and booking is recommended to avoid disappointment. The menu available every day 12–2 and 7–9.30, lists a good range of snacks such as a hot cheese and ratatouille flan and home-made soup like shellfish bisque with spicy chilli roulade and garlic croutons. Also turkey and cranberry or duck and cherry pie with salad and a mixed leaf seasonal salad with locally smoked chicken and pink grapefruit dressed with raspberry vinaigrette. In addition to daily specials like a lamb vegetable stew with dumplings other dishes on the menu include oven baked mushroom caps filled with Stilton and walnut, lightly scrambled eggs with smoked salmon, roasted rack of local lamb, oven roasted breast of guinea fowl, pan fried escalop of pork with cider and Calvados and vegetarian baked avocados filled with tomatoes and aubergines.

Weekday opening times 12–2.30 & 6–11. Sunday. 12–3 & 7–10.30.

Families welcome.

Accommodation in 7 comfortable en-suite rooms.

Telephone: (01373) 812254.

Village lies in the beautiful Wadbury Vale about three miles west of Frome.

Approximate distance: 6½ miles. OS Map 183 ST 726/491.

Ample parking at the pub and in the road at the front.

An extremely enjoyable but very demanding walk in this most beautiful area of Somerset which first follows a very attractive bridleway beside the Mells river before reaching the pretty hamlet of Great Elm. From here a woodland path guides you high up above Whatley Bottom and past Tedbury Camp leading to Whatley village. For the final section of the walk a pretty but demanding path descends to a brook and then rises up a rock strewn valley skirting the quarry before reaching Little Green. April and May is the best time but still some expect wet conditions.

Turn left then immediately left up the lane beside the pub to the church of St Andrew, go round to the back and up between the avenue of clipped yew trees to the squeeze stile, one of only three surviving examples patented and built in 1857 by Thomas Lyne of Malmesbury. Turn right and cross the field to the stile on the far side keeping straight ahead along the road to the T-junction and cross to the stone stile opposite. Bearing right walk down to the stone stile in the far hedge, turn left, cross the road and immediately join the signed bridleway on the right.

This well surfaced track rises steadily through young woodland amass with garlic ransoms, bluebells and other wild flowers also butterflies like orange tips and common blues. The path passes close to the Mells river, between many derelict dwellings and pump buildings later rising behind the buildings to meet a tarred drive. Walk for awhile and then join the footpath on the right (part of the Wyvern Way) which follow the course of the river between large areas of garlic ransoms before rising steeply to the pretty village of Great Elm.

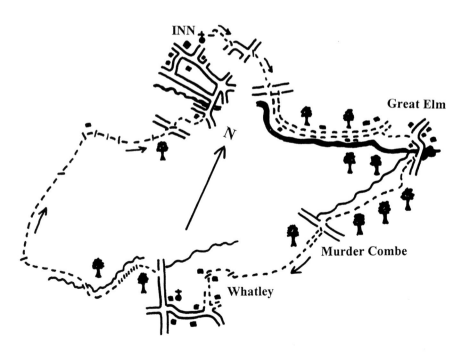

55

Great Elm

Turn right down the hill and cross the bridge. After pausing for awhile to enjoy the view across the water go through the kissing gate on the right and bear left up the narrow path through the trees turning right onto the cross path. The area is a feast for lovers of wild flowers. Look for bluebells, primroses, pink campion, arums, cow parsley, wood anemones even Solomon's seal. After rising steadily the path flattens running parallel with the river and railway line below, the only sounds to be heard are that of running water, birds and bees.

Upon reaching the road, cross over to the stile and join the footpath sign-posted, to Shepton Mallet. Go up the track, into the field and straight ahead across to the stile. The spire of Whatley church looms large ahead of you as you climb more stiles before reaching a gateway. Bear left over to the stile, up the narrow path, across the driveway to the path in the corner and out to the road.

On the right is Whatley Vineyard and Herb Garden. Well worth a visit. (Entry is free from April 1st – 30th September, Wednesday, Thursday, Friday, Saturdays and Bank Holidays from 10–1 & 2–6. Sunday 12–5. The vineyard extends to 3 acres and wine is made from 5 grape varieties. Conducted tours can be arranged for 15 or more people).

Turn right taking care until you reach the pavement, walk to the crossroads then turn right. Part way down the hill, but before reaching the quarry, look for a footpath up the bank on the left. It is signed 'perimeter path'. Further on fork right by the finger-post. After a tricky descent on some very uneven steps the path runs beside the brook before reaching a stile on the right. Cross the field to the far side and round the corner by the road then bear right up the field, across to the plank bridge in the right-hand boundary and turn left. This pretty but often muddy and demanding path rises steadily towards the road at the top. At times progress is slow over large moss covered boulders. More wild flowers are much in evidence even the occasional purple spotted orchid. Cross the stile on the right and follow the perimeter fence all the way round, over a stile midway until you reach the stile by the farm buildings. Turn right to a second stile and maintain direction following the path until you reach a stile and a small woodland path leading to the road.

Carefully cross to the stile opposite, walk down to the corner of the field, bear right down to the stile in the bottom right-hand corner and go out into the lane. Cross the bridge and either take the main road on the left back to the pub or for a more prettier route turn immediately left after the bridge following the lane until you reach the turning on the right opposite Bridge Cottage. Walk up past all the dwelling then go right at the junction back to the pub.

Notley Arms, Monksilver

Beneath the Brendon Hills lies Monksilver, a peaceful village with pretty flower covered cottages, a lovely church and a very good pub. The Notley Arms is very much part of village life with a relaxed atmosphere pervading throughout. The small side porch leads directly into the cosy, carpeted family room which has an assortment of chairs, farmhouse tables and a bookcase, whilst opposite, the main L-shaped bar has that lovely lived in feel. An interesting mix of furniture includes cosy settles, a large scrubbed farmhouse table, small mahogany tables, a piano, a bookcase, paintings on the wall, boxes of games and many interesting artefacts. Wood burning stoves are located at both ends, one set in an attractive stone walled fireplace. Outside there is a pretty sheltered garden with picnic benches.

The well stocked bar in this lovely pub presently includes, Exmoor Ale, Draught Bass, Wadworth 6X and Ushers and some good wines all at the same reasonable price (under £8 on my visit in 1997).

The inn, always busy with diners, is well known for its good food all home-cooked using fresh ingredients and available weekdays 12–2 and 7–9.30. Sunday 12–1.45 and 7–9. On my last visit I had the choice of home-made soup, coarse country pate, smoked mackerel fillet and prawns with garlic ginger or mayonnaise. There was a rich man's pouch – wholemeal pitta bread with hot garlic beef and salad and a pot of mayonnaise or poor man's pocket with cheese and beggar man's bag with bacon and mushrooms. Reasonably priced hay maker and forester's lunch are followed by lasagne, roasted aubergine with fresh apricot and mint salad, cod and asparagus strudel, plus a vegetarian special. Daily specials could include a wild mushroom strudel, home-made pasta and fresh fish with more meals in the evening. Sweets ranged from treacle tart and cream and fresh strawberry cheesecake to pear yoghurt ice-cream and fresh fruit crumble and cream.

Opening times Monday – Saturday 11.30–2.30 & 6.30–11. Sunday 12–2.30 & 7–10.30.

Families welcome, dogs inside and out.

Telephone: (01984) 656217.

Village located on the B3188 between Wiveliscombe and Washford.

Approximate distance: 3 miles. OS Map 181 ST 073/375.

Ample parking at the side of the pub and in the village.

A delightful walk at first up an attractive bridleway to Bird's Hill, one of the best bluebell woods in the area. After a short walk down an attractive lane and a descent through pretty woodland scenic field paths and a peaceful lane gently guide you back to the pub.

Leave the pub turning right and take the next lane on the right, walk a short way up the hill and join the bridleway on the left sign-posted, Colton Cross 1½. This very attractive narrow, sunken track rises steadily its steep-sided banks home to primroses, pink champion, ferns and other moisture loving plants. At one point water cascades down a slate wall swiftly taken away by a gully at one side of the path. Higher up through a gap in the path one has a good view across to Minehead. Near the top the path rises through Bird's Hill amass with bluebells in May.

Eventually when you reach the gate turn right into the lane walking down past swathes of primroses. On the left is a track the footpath is sign-posted, to Nettlecombe. Follow the track through the woods after a while looking for a path on the right, the only indication is a small yellow square on an oak tree (it is easy to miss). At first descending quite steeply through conifer trees the path flattens through broadleaf woodland with more bluebells, crosses a track and continues downhill to meet a wide gravel track (look for the occasional splash of yellow marking the way). Turn left and then immediately right along the drive walking until you reach the fingerpost.

Climb the stile into the field on the right signposted, to Monksilver. Head down and up the field to the gate maintaining direction across to the stile in the far hedge. Cross the lane to the stile opposite and walk straight ahead keeping beside the hedge, climb the stile into the adjoining field and bear left making for the stile in the opposite hedge. Turn right following this attractive peaceful lane back down towards the village. At the rear of the church is a gate and path, which leads directly round to the car park of the pub.

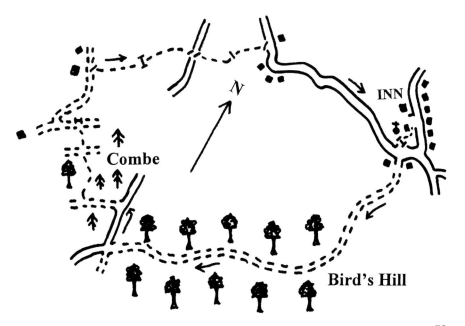

N

INN

Combe

Bird's Hill

The Kings Arms Inn, Montacute

Montacute's history can be traced back to a settlement in the 7th century and by the 9th century was known as Bishopston. A folly, built in 1760, now occupies the spot on St Michael's Hill where a castle built by Robert Count of Mortain, half brother to King William, once stood – its stones possibly used to build the priory subsequently destroyed by order of Henry VIII. Montacute House, built for Sir Edward Phelips in 1600 is one of the finest examples of an Elizabethan mansion in Britain.

Built from local golden ham stone the delightful 16th century Kings Arms Inn is sited close to the church of St. Catherine at the foot of St Michael's Hill. A warm log fire in the central wall heats both the bar and dining room.

The inn last changed hands in March 1998 and is now owned by The Old English Pub Company. The well stocked Pickwick Bar offers a good selection of drinks, an excellent wine list and two real ales, Directors drawn straight from the barrel and John Smiths on hand pump.

A very high standard of food is available at lunchtime and from 7–9, except Sunday evening. The menu which might be subject to change presently lists home-made soup of the day, Kings Arm's curry, terrine of pigeon with home-made marmalade and toast, pan fried mushrooms with black pudding and sausages in a cider sauce topped with a poached egg, a salad of celery, blue cheese and paprika roasted nuts. Also Somerset smokie on a bed of lemon dressing and salad leaves (large and small portions), thin slices of smoked duck breast served with chef's pear chutney and garnish, butterfly lamb chop pan fried with a Cumberland sauce, home-made rabbit and wild boar pie flavoured with junipers and gin and a puff pastry case filled with tagliatelle and wild mushrooms in a cream and yoghurt sauce.

The inn is open on weekdays all day 11–11.

Children in eating area and restaurant only.

En-suite bedrooms include an elegant 4-poster bed.

Telephone: (01935) 822513.

Village signed south from the A3088 4 miles west of Yeovil.

Approximate distance: 4 miles. OS Map 193 ST 496/170.

Ample free parking all along the road at the front.

An extremely enjoyable scenic walk, demanding at times from this most historic and attractive village which takes you first across farm land down to Little Norton and then high up in to the Ham Hill Country Park returning along the summit of Hedgecock Hill. Conditions underfoot are generally good and the paths are all well marked. One striking feature of the walk is the sheer number of hart's tongue ferns. Nearby Montacute House is a magnificent Elizabethan house owned by The National Trust and open to the public from March 30–November 3 daily, except Tuesdays, 12–5.30 p.m.

From the inn turn right, past the church on your left then along the private drive and up to the gate. Follow the signed bridleway ahead, uphill turning right into Hollow Lane at the top and almost immediately cross the stile into the field on the right. Turn left and, keeping close to the boundary cross a couple stiles eventually reaching a third beside the gate leading to the road.

Turn right and cross to the stile beside the gate opposite. Walk down this attractive track turning right at the cross track and climb the stile beside the gate following the sunken track round to the left and down to the stile. Proceed along the beaten path to the bottom of the field then bear right across to the stile, out onto the track and turn right.

Walk for awhile, and having passed a turning to the left look for a signed path leading up into the woods on the right. The little path snakes up the hillside under a

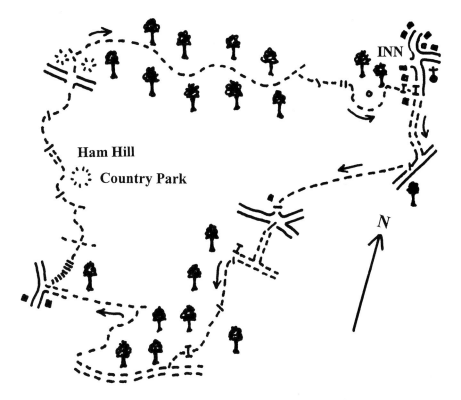

laurel arch to meet a cross path at which point turn left. Eventually, after passing a dwelling on the left, join the drive to the house, and just before reaching the lane climb the steps to the path on the right sign-posted, Ham Hill ¾. Take time to rest and look back at the view as you climb this very steep hillside. Keep straight ahead at a cross path and just before reaching the top turn left, up round to the kissing gate and onto the fort.

Walk through the enclosure bearing left to pick up the gravel path leading to the kissing gate. Keep straight ahead towards the car park then join the footpath on the right sign-posted, Stoke Sub Hamdon. Cross the road to the signed path opposite forking right at the finger post. (Thirsty? a short

diversion up the hill will bring you to the Prince of Wales). After crossing Ham Hill, extensively quarried for its stone, bear right carefully descending the steep stony bank to meet a level path beside an old stone wall and turn right.

From here simply follow the path through the trees, bearing right at the cross path then over a stile, and near the bottom fork right down to one last stile. Walk straight across to the pair of gates and turn right to pick up the path around St Michael's Hill. Head down the gully and across to the gates turning left back to the pub. All that remains of the priory built in the 16th century is the magnificent gatehouse on the right now part of Abbey Farm.

The George Inn, Norton St Philip

No book on Somerset pubs would be complete without the ancient George Inn. Built around 1227 it is one of the oldest alehouses in the country and has been quenching the thirst of travellers since that time. This remarkable inn has a timber and stone exterior and high mullioned windows. Large wooden doors guard the entrance to the cobble-stoned courtyard from which one has access to the lofty beamed bars. The lounge has a massive stone fireplace with log fire in winter and simple furnishing on the bare wood floor which consist of high back settles, pew bench seating and farmhouse tables and chairs. The bar, similar in appearance, has a unique solid wooden trestle table for dispensing drinks. Norton St Philip paid a significant part in the Monmouth Rebellion the Duke having stayed here before his forces came to grips with the royal army.

The inn is owned by Wadworth and was re-opened in October following extensive restoration. The full range of Wadworth's excellent real ales are available together with a guest ale presently Hall & Woodhouse Tanglefoot.

Very good food, available daily from 12–2.30 (3.00 Saturday/Sunday) and 6.30–9.30 (Sunday 7–9.30) consists of the usual snacks like sandwiches and ploughman's plus a range of daily specials listed on the blackboard. Presently you might expect to see a venison stew, braised pheasant, lamb tagine with couscous, lamb shanks braised in honey, orange and rosemary and an Irish stew. Heading the set menu are starters such as moules mariniere, bruschetta with parma ham and brie, smoked salmon terrine, baked avocado and prawns plus soups and chowders, followed by dishes like pigeon breast braised with button mushrooms and shallots in red wine and sizzling fajaitas. Sweets range from blueberry and brandy bread and butter pudding and crème brulee to rhubarb crumble and spotted dick. Coffees are served between 11–12 and afternoon tea from 3.

Weekday opening times 11–3 & 5.30–11. Sunday 12–3 & 7–10.30.

Families in dining room. Dogs on leads.

Accommodation in eight well appointed en-suite rooms, some four-poster beds. Telephone: (01373) 834224.

Walk No. 21

Village located on the A366 at its junction with the B3110 south of Bath.

Approximate distance: $6\frac{1}{4}$ miles. OS Map 172 ST 774/559.

Rear car park plus limited spaces in village roads.

A fairly long but enjoyable walk which heads north across fields to Hinton Charterhouse after which a bridleway leads to Cleaves Wood a haven for wildlife and flowers. Track and field paths guide you back through the little hamlet of Hassage. Although a bit strenuous in places the going generally is good underfoot.

Go out into the road and turn left and in twenty paces turn right into North Street, turn right at the junction, cross the road and join the signed footpath opposite. Bearing left walk to the stile in the far corner and continue up the drive towards Norwod Farm – a rare breed centre open to the public. Just beyond the short track cross the stile into the field on the left. After a series of stiles, negotiate a couple more beside woodland then bear right across the field making for the far corner turning right. The path not very well defined meanders though trees and scrub to reach a farm gate. Walk straight

across the field to the stile and follow the path through a strip of recently planted trees (can be come a bit overgrown in summer with lots of nettles). Leave by the stile on the far side, walk out into the lane and turn left.

Head for the road and cross into the lane opposite which soon becomes a track eventually reaching Cleaves Wood, a SSSI. Pass through the gate and fork left down across a small meadow abundant in summer with many interesting wild flowers. In evidence are large quantities of wild marjoram, scabious, centaurea – wild cornflower and hyper-

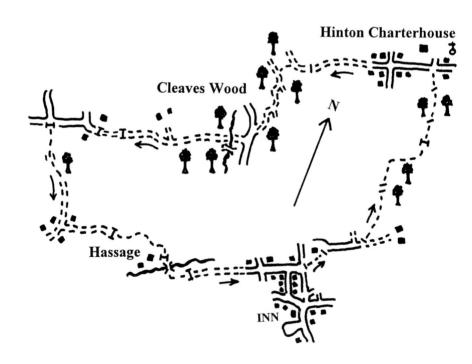

icum peforatum a member of the St John's wort family. Turn left at the bottom following the track through the bluebell wood, fork right and further on fork right again down a narrow path leading to a stile. Go over into the lane and turn left.

In a short distance take the track on the right, cross the footbridge over the stream and climb the track. This stone-surfaced bridleway rises steadily and continuously, through a couple of gates and into a field. Keep straight ahead along the gravel track, through the farmyard to the lane and turn left.

Keep walking until you reach the lane on the right at which point go into the field on the left, cross to the far side, go through the hedge gap and continue down the field to the opening in the dip opposite. Keeping close to the left-hand boundary walk to the bottom of the field and steadily climb the track opposite leading to the little hamlet of Hassage.

After passing Hassage House take the track on the left keeping straight ahead at the top of the hill and further on bear right downhill towards Mount Pleasant Farm. Go through the gate into the field and follow the hedge line down and round to the gate, cross the narrow concrete bridge, go up the bank into the field ahead and turn left. Simply follow the bridleway through a gate, down to the lane and turn left. Go over the crossroads turning right into North Street and retrace your steps back to the pub.

Hinton House

The Montague Inn, Shepton Montague

Surrounded by organic farms in a peaceful village setting the delightfully restored Montague Inn has to be one of my favourites. The friendly main bar has a nice stone fireplace with a log fire in winter, a comfortable mix of furnishings, lots of shining artefacts including a large grandfather clock. There is separate cosy non smoking dining room tastefully decorated in shades of pink which has an enormous fireplace lit with candles, rugs on the floor and a large tapestry hanging from one wall. The smaller part wood panelled 'Old Snug' is also laid for dining. The well tended rear garden and terrace enjoy an open rural aspect.

The inn is a freehouse efficiently run by the owners John and Telly White who took over in 1998. A selection of real ales served traditionally straight from the cask include Butcombe Bitter, Green King IPA and Montague Harrier.

Superb beautifully presented food, available every day (except Monday lunch) and 7.30–9 (not Sunday) is expertly prepared by Chef Rozanne Maclean trained at the famous Michelin starred, Le Mere Blanc in France. Typical at lunchtime there might be soup, a casket of kidneys in Maderia sauce, Tuscan sausages with caramelised onions, crispy cod with a basil pesto, tagliatelle a la cabenera, crab cakes and chicken breast with oregano. There is an interesting set menu in the evening, which is changed regularly. On my visit there were four starters which included delicate tomato mousse with thyme and basil on a raw tomato coulis and spider crab on linguine pasta with a chilli and parsley sauce followed by roast breast of guinea fowl on a chervil sauce with asparagus, loin of lamb fillet with a light curry sabayon and basil jus and roast duckling breast on a corn syrup sauce with a croustillant of onions and coriander. Puddings like chocolate terrine, Grand Marnier creme brulee and orange tart are a perfect end to your meal.

Three stylish en-suite bedrooms.

Weekday opening times 12–3 (closed Monday lunchtime) & 6–11. Sunday 12–3 & 7–10.30.

Families welcome, dogs in bar.

Telephone/Fax: (01749) 813213.

Village signed from both the A359 and A371 approximately $3\frac{1}{2}$ miles Northwest from Wincanton.

Approximate distance: 4 miles. OS Map 183 ST 674/315.

Large car park beside the inn.

An interesting scenic walk at first along a track and across fields leading to the 13th century church of St Peter. Sadly it was completely destroyed by fire in 1964, only the walls and the tower remained but happily restoration was undertaken and completed in 1966. After following a narrow path beside a stream you are guided towards Pitcombe Church and high up onto old drove tracks before returning past the rear entrance to Hadspen House where a permissive circular path has been laid out through the park.

Leave the pub turning left, go down through the village and take the next left, up the hill and just past the new dwelling turn left onto the gravel track. Where it veers right cross the stile into the field on the left keeping straight ahead to the hedge opposite then turn right and walk to the far corner. Climb down the bank to the stile and head across the field beside the hedge on the right. Go through the gap and along the escarpment eventually bearing left down to the stile beside the gate turning right into the lane.

Walk as far as the church then join the little path at the rear which leads to the lane. Bear left between the buildings and turn left at the junction. Soon there is a stile on the right, cross into the field and bear right down to the stile in the far corner. Turn left, yomp the stream bearing right around the hillside keeping to a line fairly close to the old railway line, make for the gap by the stream (can be wet) then keep straight ahead to the stile in the corner. Proceed along this narrow path, which winds its way though a newly planted area beside the stream eventually reaching the road at a gap in the wall (can become a bit overgrown in summer).

Turn right then immediately left on the road to Pitcombe. Further ahead take the lane on the left leading to the church and join the track at the rear. Walk steadily uphill until you reach the stile on the right then bear left climbing steeply up the field between the two hills making for the stile in

the far top corner, go over onto the track and turn left.

Turn left when you reach the crosstrack and at the road carefully cross to the lane opposite. On the bend is the entrance to Hadspen House. The parkland is managed by The Countryside Stewardship and a permissive circular path has been set up, details are displayed on the gate. The gardens of the house, which are laid out in colour themed beds and open to the public for a fee, are well worth a visit. After this optional diversion continue following the lane round to meet the road then turn left up the hill to the pub.

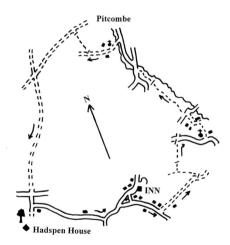

PERMISSIVE PATH NETWORK THROUGH HADSPEN HOUSE PARK
SHOWN OVERLEAF

CONSERVATION WALKS

The network of permissive footpaths provides an opportunity to wander through this 18th Century historic park and woodland which has remained in the possession of the present family since 1785. It is now being restored to its original design with the help of Countryside Stewardship. There are excellent views of the parkland on the walk and two newly restored ponds can be seen. Please close any gates which you pass through. It is also possible to visit the renowned Hadspen walled ornamental garden. (Admission to the walled garden is chargeable as it is under separate management).

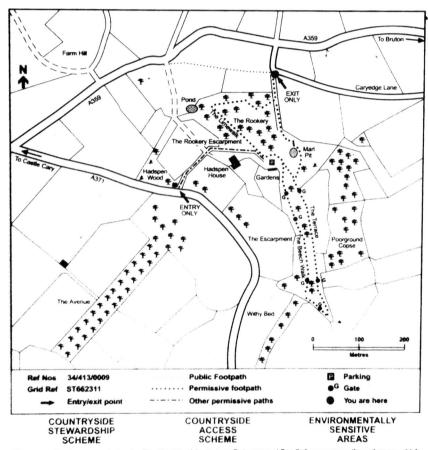

Ref Nos	34/413/0009	.... Public Footpath	🅿 Parking
Grid Ref	ST662311	.... Permissive footpath	●G Gate
➡	Entry/exit point	—·—·— Other permissive paths	● You are here

| COUNTRYSIDE STEWARDSHIP SCHEME | COUNTRYSIDE ACCESS SCHEME | ENVIRONMENTALLY SENSITIVE AREAS |

This access has been provided under The Ministry of Agriculture Fisheries and Food's farm conservation schemes, which help farmers and land managers protect and improve the countryside, its wildlife and history. It is permissive access and no new rights of way are being created. Existing rights of way are not affected. Please follow the Country Code and observe any other requirements shown above. Do not disturb wildlife, livestock or other visitors and in particular keep dogs under control. This is working farmland so please take care, people using this site do so at their own risk.

The Greyhound Inn, Staple Fitzpaine

Resplendently draped in summer with colourful climbers this attractive stone inn started life as a hunting lodge for the Portman family and only became an inn some 150 years ago. The bar at the front still retains a lovely flagstone floor, a large brick fireplace with wood burning stove and part wood panelled walls. Furnishings consist of a mix of settles, padded barrel stools and solid wooden tables. Two similar rooms are set for dining and there is a larger family room at the back, a skittle alley that doubles as a function room and bench seats at the front.

This well managed inn last changed hands in June 1998 and is now part of Lionhart a small pub chain. The well stocked bar includes up to six real ales, one tapped straight from the cask, the choice usually between Otter Bright, Tanglefoot, Exmoor Ale and Exmoor Fox, London Pride and Draught Bass.

All food, presently available 12–2.30 and 6.30–10 is freshly prepared and cooked on the premises. Diners can chose something from the bar menu like home-made soup, ploughman's, salads and sandwiches also sausage of the day with mash, ham, egg and chips, bread-crumbed plaice and chips, supreme of chicken filled with garlic butter and vegetable lasagne. More elaborate dishes might include smoked haddock poached on a bed of spinach and wild boar and juniper berry terrine followed by rainbow trout lightly grilled and enriched with prawns and mushrooms, pink breast of duck smothered with black cherries and red wine sauce, rack of English lamb also calves liver or fresh tuna steak both sauteed in parsley butter. There are meals for children and vegetarian dishes like vegetable crumble and a mixed bean and spicy chick pea and vegetable hot pot. Thursday night is music night.

Weekday opening times Monday – Friday 12–3 & 5–11. Saturday 11–11. Sunday presently 12–3 & 7–10.30.

Families in dining areas, dogs in front bar only with permission.

Four en-suite rooms to be available in near future.

Telephone: (01823) 480227.

71

Walk No. 23

Village signed off the A358 between Ilminster and Taunton.

Approximate distance: $5\frac{1}{4}$ miles. OS Map 193 ST 264/184.

Good parking at the pub alternatively park by the church in the lane opposite leading to Bow Green.

An enjoyable scenic walk strenuous but not over demanding at first on field paths leading to Thurlbear Wood Nature Reserve after which your route leads to Netherclay and beyond onto a rising bridleway through attractive woodland. The area is poorly drained and very muddy in the winter best time is the summer.

Turn right from the pub and keep to the right-hand side carefully walk up the hill, past the trees on the left and at the top go through the gate into the field on the right. Bearing left walk down to the gap in the far corner then head across the field to the stile in the hedge opposite. Bearing right walk to the access point into the field ahead, up the field and through the gap into the field on the right. Turn left up to the gate and into the lane.

Turn left and in a few paces enter the field on the right and walk down to the gap in the far right-hand corner then bear slightly left up to the gap in the hedge. Turn left entering the adjoining field by the oaks then bear left across to the gate, left of the dwelling turning right into the lane.

Walk up and round towards Slough Green but before reaching the junction and The Farmers Arms, take the Forestry track on the left into Thurlbear Wood. Managed by the Somerset Wildlife Trust the reserve, which covers about 16 ha lies on a low plateau of Trissiac limestone and shale which unfortunately for the walker makes

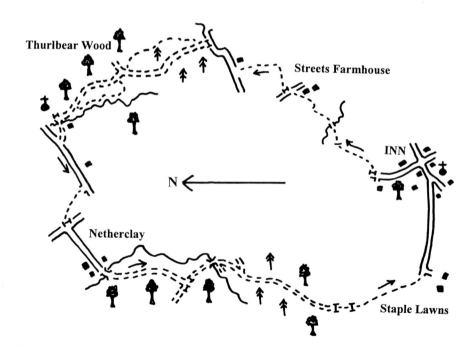

72

for bad drainage. The reserve is home to many butterflies, birds and wild flowers. Look for some bluebells, garlic ransoms, wood spurge, sweet woodruff and early purple orchids. Having entered the wood you can follow a signed path on the right through the trees otherwise keep to the main track which doglegs right before reaching the junction of the footpath from the right and two often muddy tracks. Take the one on the left or follow the narrow path on the left, which snakes through the trees close to the stream re-joining the track further on. Carry on up to the cross track, turn left, cross the stream by the dwelling, go out into the lane and turn left.

Just before reaching the junction take the signed path on the right, (merely shortcuts the corner). Leave by the gate and cross into the lane opposite leading to Netherclay. Walk past all the dwellings, go over the stream and join the track, which bears left and rises steadily beside woodland. Further on fork left and when you reach the entrance to a wood go through the small gate on the left, following the path through the trees. After crossing the bridge, ignore the first track on the right but keep straight ahead on the wide gravel track which bears right rising steadily before turning sharply left at which point keep straight ahead onto the narrow gravel and mud track.

As you climb it narrows to the width of a footpath before reaching a farm gate. Cross to the gate opposite, pass through into the field and bear left over and down towards the farm buildings and out onto the drive. keep straight ahead along the lane back past the church to the pub. St Peter's was rebuilt in the 15th century on the site of a 12th century church. The south isle was added in 1841.

Thurlbear

The Rose & Crown, Stoke St Gregory

There is a real homely feel about this warm and welcoming family run pub, which is now hidden behind a high hedge. The structure of the building dates back to the late 1700's and was sold in 1839 for £56.10/-. It became an inn in 1867 and has had numerous landlords since that time, the longest period held by Mr & Mrs Dyer from 1861 till 1904. The nicely cluttered, cosy back bar has assorted seating with some intimate high back settles, lots of paper cuttings and posters stuck in the space between the ceiling beams. One interesting feature is a 60 foot illuminated well, rediscovered in 1982, it served the pub with fresh water until 1948. There is a comfortable side room with a large fireplace (not in use at present), candle topped tables in the smart sunny front dining room which has wildlife paintings on the wall. For fine weather drinkers there are picnic benches in the front garden. The owners ask you not to be afraid of their ghost 'Bonnie' seen dressed in light grey and wearing a bonnet.

Formally owned by the Brutton Brewery then by Bass, the present owners, Ron and Ireen Browning purchased the pub in 1979. Real ales presently available are Royal Oak, Hardy Bitter and Withy Cutter from the local Moor Beer Company.

Good food is available every day 12.30–2 and 7–10. Included in the lunch time bar menu are soup and ploughman's plus grilled kidneys and bacon, scrumpy chicken, grilled skate wings and Dover sole whilst those partaking in the three course dinner have a choice of 23 starters! There is a cornet of ham, mussels in garlic, hot grapefruit with ginger wine, stuffed Burgundy snails and lobster soup with brandy. To follow fish dishes such as grilled whole Brixham plaice and Scotch salmon hollandaise. Tournedos Rossini, roast rack of lamb, supreme of chicken Stilton, Chateaubriand (2 persons), baked chicken with brie and roast duckling a l'orange are listed as are vegetarian meals.

Weekday opening times are from 11–3 & 7–11. Sunday 12–3 & 7–10.30.

Children and dogs equally welcome.

Overnight accommodation is available. One double and two twins in cottage annexe.

Telephone: (01823) 490296.

Village is signed from the A378 just past its junction with the A358 Langport road Southeast of Taunton. Pass through North Curry enter Stoke, bear right past the church eventually reaching the pub on the left (easily missed behind a high hedge)

Approximate distance: 4 miles. OS Map 193 ST 354/274.

Parking for about 14 cars at the pub plus ample room in the lane.

This area is known as 'The Moors' it is fertile land providing grazing in summer but largely covered with water and inaccessible in winter. This is the landscape that gave Somerset its name, 'the land of summer'. The conditions here are ideal for growing willow and led to basket making one of Somerset's oldest industries and although once employing hundreds of people is happily experiencing a revival. Our walk at first follows a path across historic Sedge Moor then passes beside two factories still in production, crosses Cames Mead then follows the River Tone for a short distance before returning on a series of field paths. Fairly level the going is mostly good underfoot but best walked in summer. P H Coate & Son at Meare Green Court has a visitor centre, museum and shop open Monday – Saturday 9–5. Guided tours are available at half-hourly intervals, Monday – Friday 10–4 covering all aspects of the industry. The walk continues across Cames Mead beside the River Tone returning to the pub along a series of field paths.

Turn right out of the pub back down the lane then go left into Windmill Lane. Walk to the end and enter the field on the right (waymarked). Keep straight ahead close to

the hedge on the right eventually reaching a gap in the hedge and a stile leading to a field. Turn immediately left over a second stile and maintain direction towards the far stile walking beside Sedgemoor Old Rhyne. Climb another stile then bear right across the field to the stile in the hedge, turn right walk up the field to the gate, go left of the farm following the track up to the lane and turn right.

Round the next bend, cross the stile into the field on the left and walk up to the stile at the top. Keep straight head negotiating two more crossing points before reaching a gate allowing access to the road. Turn right and almost immediately left entering the premises of P.H.Coate & Son. Keep straight ahead past the factory and car park beyond, crossing the stile beside the gate and along the fenced track to the next gate. The track leads down to gate at the bottom. Pass through making for the gate and plank bridge, climb the bank of the River Tone, cross the stile and continue ahead towards the bridge bearing right past the dwellings then next left to reach the lane.

Take the next left, past another willow factory and upon reaching an old barn turn right through a couple of farm gates, enter the field and turn left. Pass through the gate and turn right making for the gate in the far hedge. Bearing slightly left head up to the gate, over a couple of crossing points, climbing one last stile then walk across to the gate turning left into the lane.

Keep walking until you reach a signed footpath on the right, cross the stile into the field, walk to the stile on the far side and join the path into the housing estate following the road round and down to the lane then turn left.

Proceed until you reach a small wooden gate on the right then follow the well maintained path behind the new houses and over the crossing point into the field keeping straight ahead, over two more stiles turning left into the lane back to the pub.

The Blue Ball Inn, Triscombe

Peacefully located in a narrow lane beneath the Quantock Hills this attractive two-story thatched country pub dates from around 1766. Originally three cottages the seated entrance porch leads directly into the warm and comfortable main, low beamed bar which features a large inglenook fireplace and warm wood burning stove. Furnishings consist of country style tables, chairs and wooden settles. The recent addition of a conservatory has increased the dining area with more chairs and tables positioned in the attractive terraced garden with views over the Vale of Taunton. The Blue Ball is probably one of few pubs in the country that has separate thatched toilets

The pub is a freehouse well run by the owners Sally and Paddy Groves. In the bar there is a good choice of fine wines plus three real ales namely Cotleigh Tawny Bitter plus a couple of guests like Brains SA Best Bitter and Otter Ale.

Good home-cooked quality food is served weekdays 12–1.45 and 7–9.30, Sunday 12–2 and 7–9. A selection of starters presently listed on the menu include brie and salmon parcels, grilled goats cheese and chicken and avocado salad followed by monkfish with saffron and Pernod, fillet steak with Stilton and bacon, escalope of venison with port and juniper berries and grilled tuna with peppers and onions. At lunchtime you might find available a selection of specials like haddock mornay, fresh crab salad, home-made pies and grilled whole Torbay sole. Sweet lovers have a choice of home-made puds such as hazelnut pavlova with toffee sauce, chocolate and brandy torte and bramley apple pie.

Weekday opening times 12–2.30 & 7–11.30. Sunday 12–3 & 7–10.30.

Children welcome dogs if clean and well behaved.

Telephone: (01984) 618242.

Walk No. 25

The tiny hamlet of Triscombe is signed off the A358 north of Taunton.

Approximate distance: $4\frac{1}{4}$ miles. OS Map 181 ST 156/355.

Car park opposite also space in the lane at the front.

Steep in places and a little demanding this delightful scenic and often bracing walk takes you high up onto the Quantock Hills. The going is generally good underfoot mostly on stone-surfaced bridleways and grass covered paths.

Leave the pub turning right, walk a short distance up the hill and take the next right behind the pub. Follow the lane up and round then take the gravel track on the left. Further on fork right onto the narrow signed bridleway walking until you reach a cross track at which point turn left. Uneven in places the path rises very steeply through mixed woodland before reaching the moor at the top.

Turn left by the dew pond and follow this scenic track up Wills Neck forking right at the trig. point. The track descends gradually to a cross track at which point turn left.

Keep straight ahead past the car park and Triscombe Stone walking for a further half mile through this attractive woodland strip until you reach the signed bridleway on the left.

Pass through the gate and join the gully down the hillside and just before reaching the gate near the bottom join the signed footpath on the left. Although steep at first it soon levels before reaching a gate then gradually descends through attractive mixed woodland. Turn right at the cross track then left back to the pub.

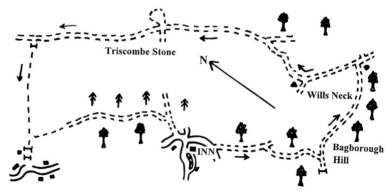

The Cotley Inn, Wambrook

Few places remain in England where one can still find perfect peace and tranquility – Wambrook is one such village its pub occupying a sunny position overlooking the pretty valley and church below. This welcoming stone-built inn comprises several linked rooms providing accommodation for quiet dining, general drinking or the playing of pub games like skittles. One dividing wall houses a wood burning stove whilst the furthermost of the the two cosy non-smoking dining rooms has a very attractive inglenook fireplace. Paintings and corn dollies displayed on the walls are priced for sale. Outside there are picnic benches in the large, low-walled beer garden.

The inn is a freehouse well run by the owners David & Sue Livingstone. On offer is a good choice of drinks plus two real ales presently, Otter Ale and Flowers Original.

A good range of imaginative bar meals which can be ordered daily 11.30–2.30 and 7–10 (Sunday 12–2) include home-made soup, creamed mushrooms with tarragon, lamb kidneys in port and cream and mushroom fritters with garlic mayonnaise. In addition there is chicken sautéed in a ginger and pumpkin sauce, chicken in sherry, mushrooms and cream, cordon bleu, sweet and sour or curried. 'Big fishy eats' include baked plaice with dill and tarragon, seafood gratin with rice and salad and salmon steak with white wine and tarragon. 'Big meaty eats' include a good range of grills like a rump steak with a borderlaise or Stilton sauce, devilled kidneys with rice and Cotley mixed grill. Vegetarians can choose between creamed mushrooms with rice and salad, mushrooms stuffed with spinach, tomato, rice and salad, brie parcels with a fruit sauce and vegetable and Stilton crumble. On my last visit blackboard specials included chicken and gammon pie and trout fillets.

Weekday opening times 11.30–3 & 7–11. Sunday 12–3 & 7–11.

Bed and breakfast is available offering a choice of two rooms.

Children in dining areas. Dogs welcome inside and out.

Telephone/fax: (01460) 62348

Walk No. 26

Follow village signs south from the A30 west of Chard.

Approximate distance: 2½ miles. OS Map 193 ST 296/077.

Parking at the pub or in the lane.

A short but very enjoyable walk in this remote and peaceful area of Somerset at first along an undulating farm road into a small bluebell wood then down across farm land before returning along an attractive track which climbs steadily to the village. Mostly good underfoot spring or summer is the best time to walk. Ancient oak stocks can be seen standing against the north wall of the 13th century church.

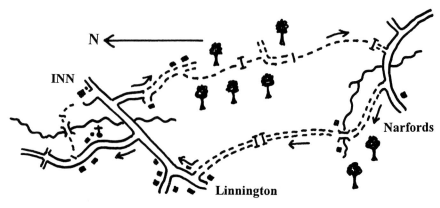

Leave the pub turning right into the lane then next left past the cottages. Further on fork left on the concrete farm road which rises steeply to a house on the left at which point take the path on the right down into the wood. Later leave by the gate into the field then fork right on the track, down to another gate, enter the field and bear right making your way down to the gate in the far corner, go out into the lane and turn right.

Cross the brook and immediately turn right and join the gravel track. Upon reaching the cottages turn right across the brook and head up the stony track – home to many wild flowers and ferns. Pass through a couple of farm gates and rejoin the track then right at the driveway to Oatlands Farm before reaching the lane.

Walk downhill then take the next left, past the church of St Mary the Virgin. Dedicated in 1362, it is built from ham stone rubble with ashlar dressings and although once thatched was leaded by 1613. Continue walking beyond the dwellings until you reach a wooden stile on the right then cross into the field and bear right down to the brook, over the plank bridge, up the bank opposite joining the path which leads to a stile and narrow path back to the pub.

The Rock Inn, Waterrow

This pretty 400 year old photogenic inn occupies a lovely spot overlooking the River Tone. It is aptly named being actually built into the rock, part of which is visible in the beamed bar beside the large attractive stone fireplace. Assorted furniture on the part wood and part carpeted floor include comfortable arm chairs and a settle beside the warm log fire. There is an attractive dining room on a slightly higher level with seating for about twenty-four.

The inn is a freehouse personally run by the owner "Brough" who on his own admission and, according to the locals, is reputed to be 'Somerset's most miserable landlord'. Two real ales presently available include Cotleigh Tawny and Exmoor Gold.

The reasonably priced bar menu, available every day of the week 11–3 and 6–11. Sunday 12–3 and 7–10.30, lists soup, baked jacket potatoes, sandwiches and ploughman's plus cottage pie, steak sandwich, curries, fish and a good choice of vegetarian dishes such as vegetable crumble, creamy vegetable Kiev with garlic sauce, tomato & vegetable tagliatelle and a vegetable curry. Also listed are chicken mascarpone and ham and basil cappelletti, home-made steak and kidney, and game or turkey pies. Whole mussels in garlic and wine sauce and three deep fried cheeses are two of the fourteen starters on the restaurant menu followed by various grills, poultry and fish like salmon paupiette with wild mushroom and wine sauce, poached halibut steak and grilled whole lemon sole. Specialities include cassoulet – French style casserole with Toulouse sausage, duck confit, haricot beans and lamb in a rich sauce and tournedos Rossini. A large sweet menu ranges from steamed puddings, pies and Salcombe dairy ice creams to specialities such as compote of green figs with cream and brandy and crepes suzettes with Grand Marnier.

No objection to dogs or children.

Weekday opening times 11–3 & 6–11. Sunday 12–3 & 7–10.30.

Seven double en-suite rooms.

Telephone: (01984) 623293.

Inn located by the bridge at Waterrow on the B3227 (formerly the A361) 14 miles west of Taunton in the Brendon foothills.

Approximate distance: 3 miles. OS Map 181 ST 052/255.

Small car park beside the inn and another opposite.

A moderately strenuous but very scenic walk on field paths, bridle tracks and peaceful country lanes. It is especially pretty in early summer when the roadside wild flowers are at their best.

From the pub turn left up the hill towards Chipstable and soon take the next left. Steadily climb this steep flower-filled lane until you reach a path on the right (can be concealed in summer). Follow the narrow track down to the gate, cross the stream and bear right picking up the grass primrose-lined path, which rises steadily to a farm gate. Continue following the path ahead making for the farm buildings and gate at the top. Go up the track, between the buildings and turn right through the farm gate. Walk across the field to the gate in the far corner than bear left across the field to the metal farm gate. Bearing left walk over

the rise and down the field making for Trowell Farm. Pass through the gate, turn right in front of the cottage, down the lane and into the field on the left. Walk round beside the hedge to the gate, go into the adjoining field and bear right down across both fields making for the stile in the far bottom corner.

Turn left into the lane, forking right at the junction. Rising through attractive woodland the verges of which are amass with wild flowers in early summer this peaceful lane eventually leads to Chipstable. After passing a dwelling on the right, but before reaching the village take the signed

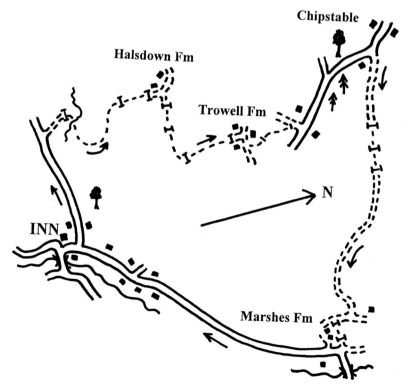

bridleway on the right. Climb this grass centred gravel track to the gate, through the gate opposite maintaining direction down to a third gate.

Rejoin this very attractive narrow track, often a little mudddy in places, which descends steadily towards the valley. At the junction turn right and, in a few steps look for the small gate on the left marked with blue on one post. Go down the short track to the gate and turn right into the lane. A pleasant stroll of about ¾ of a mile will eventually bring you directly back to the inn.

Trowell Farm

Crossways Inn, West Huntspill

This ancient coaching inn lies on the old Bridgwater to Weston Super Mare road just far enough away from the M5. A relaxing much lived-in atmosphere pervades throughout the inn, which still has old sash windows and part wood panelled walls. A large fireplace in the central bar has built-in seating, an assortment of chairs, high back settles and tables, some of scrubbed pine. One fireplace has a warm wood burning stove. There is a family room and small safe rear garden.

The inn is a freehouse well managed and run by Anne and Mick Ronca. Six real ales are always available on tap three regulars and three guests, which might include Royal Oak, Flowers Original, Flowers IPA, Brains SA Best and Triple Hop from Castle Eden.

Very good food available 12–3 and 6.30–9.30 (10 Friday & Saturday). Sunday 7–9 could include home-made soup, garlic mushrooms, ploughman's, also chicken and ham mornay, ham and prawn mornay, ham and mushroom tagliatelle, lasagne, local faggots with marrow fat peas and a beef Madras curry with poppadoms. Vegetarian dishes range from mushroom stroganoff and vegetable bake to macaroni cheese and curried nut roast. Daily specials chalked on the board might include broccoli and apple soup, celery and Stilton soup and hunter's pate followed by Stilton and leek quiche, ham and mushroom tagliatelle and beef stroganoff, plus old favourites like moussaka, chilli, beef and Guinness pie, liver and bacon casserole, cottage pie, steak and kidney and char-grilled steaks. For vegetarians cashew nut mousakka. There is a separate menu for children and tempting treacle tart, chocolate biscuit fruit slice, chocolate pudding and rhubarb and orange pie, for the sweet toothed.

Overnight accommodation, single and double rooms.

Opening times 10.30–3 & 5.30–11. Sunday 12–3 & 7–10.30.

Families welcome, dogs on a lead.

Telephone: (01278) 783756.

Walk No. 28

Pub located on the A38 south of Burnham on Sea at the junction for East Huntspill.

Approximate distance: 5 miles. OS Map 182 ST 311/453.

Park in the lane at the front, the pub's own car park or Church Road opposite.

A very enjoyable, scenic and often bracing level walk across farm land down to the shore line which follows a path beside Stockland Reach then inland alongside the estuary to Highbridge returning along a maze of field and urban paths.

From the pub cross the main road turning left and go immediately right into Church Road. Walk down to the church, enter the grounds and keeping to the right of the church walk round to the back and through the kissing gate into the field. Keep straight ahead to the stile in the far hedge, cross the track and plank bridge into the field opposite and continue ahead beside the ditch then cross the concrete bridge. Bear half right to the far side of the field making for the stile and plank bridge then cross into the lane and turn left.

Walk to the end then pass through the gate into the field ahead and continue in the same direction. Just before reaching the gate look for a plank bridge on the left, pass into the adjoining field and turn right walking round close to the hedge, leave by the stile turning right onto the tarred lane.

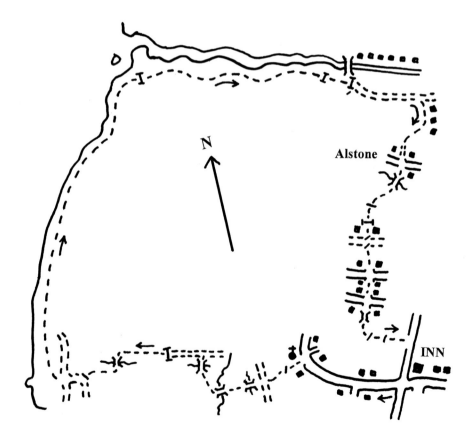

Climb the raised bank keeping to the path on the top or walk along the edge of the sea wall. Keep a look out for the many sea birds and waders especially at low tide also for various sea plants growing in the blocks including marsh samphire a tasty addition to a seafood stir fry. Walk as far as the stile then continue along the grass path beside the estuary, crossing a couple more stiles before reaching the bridge with the sea locks. Keep straight ahead onto the field path beside the canal walking to the far side turning right behind the houses. Keep to the fence line until you reach the stile then follow the path between the houses and out into the road.

Join the footpath opposite to the right of the telephone box, cross the road, go through the gate and over the stile into the field. Keep straight ahead to the ditch, cross the plank bridge into the field and bear right over to the stile in the far hedge. After passing through a plantation of young trees go through both gates, down between the barns and across the farm track to the stiles opposite. Maintain direction across to a stile in the far hedge then continue ahead to the stile beside the gate. Climb into the lane turning left, cross the road and wooden crossing point to join the path between the dwellings, cross the next road and plank bridge into the field walking to the far left-hand corner. Go over the stile and follow the path beside the ditch, over one last stile, out into the road turning right walking the short distance back to the pub.

Royal Oak Inn, Winsford

An enjoyable drive along the wooded river valley of the Exe brings you to Winsford, the village described in 1909 by W H Hudson as 'fragrant, cool, grey/green – immemorial peace – second to no English village in beauty, running waters, stone thatched cottages, hoary church tower'.

Standing opposite an ancient cobble-stoned packhorse bridge is the resplendent Royal Oak. Built in the 12th century but recently re-thatched and re-built after a disastrous fire in 1995. Two part panelled walled bars with low ceilings radiate off the front entrance both having large original open stone fireplaces with warm winter log fires. The furnishings are a mix of stick back chairs, padded window seating, wall settles and cosy partitioned seating. There is a separate very attractive restaurant and beer garden.

Real ales like Shephard & Neame's Spitfire, Exmoor Ale, Flowers IPA and Original are still served traditionally in this freehouse, straight from the cask.

Food is available everyday 12–2 and 7–9. From the set menu one could choose to start with home-made soup, deep fried tiger prawns in filo pastry, chef's homemade smooth chicken liver pate with shallot confit and a very good ploughman's, also open croissant sandwiches, a turkey, apricot and asparagus pie topped with cheese and poached fillet of salmon with horseradish cream. The main menu lists imaginative starters like polenta and poached quail's egg salad, pan fried calves liver on spring onion mashed potatoes with a rich cider jus and a terrine of vegetable mousses with a spicy tomato relish followed by char-grilled fillet of sea bass on a tower ratatouille, rosettes of venison with roasted cloves of garlic and redcurrant sauce and pan fried breast of goose with spinach puree and Marsala sauce.

Weekday opening times 11.15–3 & 6–11. Sunday 12–3 & 7–11.

Children and dogs equally welcome.

Accommodation is available in a choice of twin bedded, double or four poster rooms.

Telephone: (01643) 851455. Fax (01643) 8511009.

The pretty village of Winsford, a magnet for tourists, lies in the Exe Valley in the shadow of Winsford Hill. It is well signed from the A396.

Approximate distance: 5 miles. OS Map 181 SS 906/348.

Park close to the pub or in public car park opposite the garage.

A very scenic and extremely enjoyable but demanding walk which takes you across farm land high up onto Exmoor, circumventing the Punchbowl to reach Winsford Hill then returning through delightful woodland and along a pretty bridleway track.

From the pub turn right, walk past the war memorial then turn left crossing the bridge next to the ford. Head up the lane until you reach the gate on the left footpath signposted, to Winsford Hill via Punchbowl 2. Cross the stile on the right and keep to the narrow path behind the dwellings, over a couple more stiles and into the field. Continue ahead through a series of gates then bear left between the farm buildings following the track to the gate. Head up the field climbing steeply to the gate, go through into the adjoining field and continue ahead towards the wooden gate. Make your way up the moor on the wide grass strip taking time to look back and enjoy the view. At the top go round the rim of the Punchbowl (magnificent views) and keep straight-ahead on the wide grass track. Further on cross the grass track and continue ahead down towards the road turning right opposite the dwelling.

Cross over and follow the verge walking until you reach the gate and signed bridleway on the left. The well-trodden path crosses an area known as The Allotment arriving at a gate on the far side. Pass

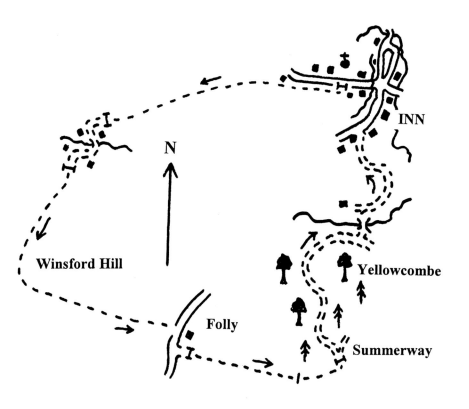

91

through and keep straight ahead close to the left-hand boundary and upon reaching the fingerpost turn left through the gate and immediately fork left. Take care when wet, the path is very steep and narrow at first before widening near the bottom. Keep to the bridleway following the blue waymarks leading down to the bridge at Yellowcombe (very picturesque). Cross the stream and stile and turn right along the narrow track. Very peaceful, attractive and uneven in places it snakes an undulating path to the village. Turn right into the lane back to the pub.

The Punchbowl

Yellowcombe

The Royal Oak Inn, Withypool

Peacefully located in the centre of Exmoor, Withypool is ideally situated for exploring the area. For nearly three centuries the Royal Oak has provided refreshment for many travellers not least R D Blackmore, who stayed here in 1866 whilst writing his novel Lorna Doone. Set on a hillside in a sunny position this two-storey inn brims with character. This is hunting country evidence of which can be seen around the walls in the many stag horns, stuffed fish and hunting prints. The 'Residents Bar' heated in winter by a warm log fire in a raised grate in the large slate built open fireplace has a beamed ceiling and an impressive large wooden settle opposite the bar. The 'Rod Room Bar' mellow with age also has a beamed ceiling, small open fireplace, a part quarry tiled floor, scrubbed wooden tables and benches. There is a separate attractive dining room with a large red brick fireplace and sought after seating on the sunny front terrace.

This well run freehouse presently offers two real ales, Exmoor Ale and Fox.

All bar meals are cooked to order and served daily 12–2 and 6.30–9.30 (Sunday 7). Apart from daily fresh fish specials and the usual snacks like home-made soup, sandwiches, ploughman's and jacket potatoes with fillings such as Stilton and asparagus the menu also lists a mixed cheese and broccoli pasta. There are various grills, half a crispy duck, two large bacon and venison farmhouse sausages, and home-cooked ham with free-range eggs. The comprehensive table d'hote and a la carte meals include starters like oven baked artichokes, filled with Somerset camembert, served with a tomato salad and basil dressing and Capricorn cheese stuffed with a cranberry sauce and roasted in breadcrumbs followed by supreme of chicken in white wine, garlic, onions, mushrooms and tomatoes and ragout of venison, pan fried with bacon, shallots and apricots.

Children and dogs in one bar only.

Weekday opening times 11–2.30 & 6–11. Sunday 12–3 & 7–11.

Overnight accommodation available in 8 rooms, 7 en-suite 1 private bath. Also 2 bed-roomed cottage self-catering or B&B.

Telephone: (01643) 831506/7 Fax: (01643) 831659.

Walk No. 30

Village signed off the B3223, south of Exford.

Approximate distance: 7½ miles. OS Map 181 SS 848/357.

There is a small car park beside the inn and ample space in the road at the front.

A long and fairly demanding walk best suited to the fitter members of the family. Four glorious miles along the River Barle bring you to Liscombe where refreshment is at hand. After crossing the famous Tarr Steps one of the finest prehistoric stone bridges the return route is up a very steep bridle track, on field paths and along the Two Moors Way, skirting Withypool Hill. There is an optional short walk for the less energetic.

Turn left from the inn, down and up the lane walking until you reach the stile on the right. Follow this permissive path round the hillside, over the stile and down to meet the river. For a very short walk you can cross on the steeping stones (water level permitting) returning along the bridleway track. The route to Tarr Steps is long, very scenic and very picturesque with many wild flowers. It is well signed with little or no explanation necessary. After passing an attractive bluebell wood bear right in the direction of the fingerpost and continue along the path forking right after a couple of miles onto the signed footpath leading to Tarr Steps. Tarr Farm on the hill is a very good 16th century inn and tea-rooms.

Cross the river and immediately bear right up the tarred drive, bridleway signposted, to Withypool Hill. The track rises very steeply to a gate then follows the hedge around the field and up to the gate at the top. Keep straight ahead walking until you reach Parsonage Farm turning right in front of the gate. Climb the sunken track, pass through a couple of gates (ignore the stile on the left) and continue following the grass covered path which leads to Westwater Farm. Go through the gate into the lane and turn right.

After crossing the bridge the wild flower filled lane rises very steeply to a cattle grid leading to the Two Moors Way. Keep straight ahead for just over a mile before crossing the Barle and arriving back to the village.

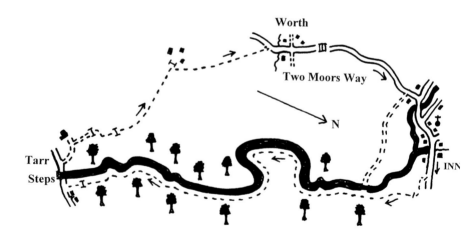

Withypool

Tarr Steps

Walk No. 30

River Barle